THE FOG

Get out of the Boat and Discover an Extraordinary Life!

Steve Laidlow

Editing and additional content by Andi Robinson

Matthew 14:28–29

What people are saying about...

THE FOG

'*A good man brings good things out of the good stored up in him.*' (*Matthew 12.35*)

'This scripture sums up this book. It's the personal fruit of a life that since meeting Jesus has been poured out in service to others and the kingdom of God. These pages are not cold, untested theology that has been learnt sat behind a desk, but instead are living principles that have been forged in the testing of pain, personal tragedy and many miraculous moments. In these pages you will find hope, challenge and inspiration and I know it will leave you encouraged in your journey, whether you are just starting out, or have been on the road for many years.

God Bless'

Pastor Derek Martin Smith, Senior Pastor, Kings Church

'A man of action, a man of faith - that's who Pastor Steve is, for I have personally witnessed the fruits of what he has shared in this book. Every time I have an opportunity to work closely with him, I am still learning and being inspired by how he "walks the talk." I commend you for deciding to read this book. Get ready to be activated into the plan of God. Your life will never be the same again!'

Pastor Sam Sisson, Living Faith International Church, West Jakarta, Indonesia

'Steve Laidlow is a hard-working person with deep passion for His work and a big vision. To this day I remember his famous quote when I rented him his church's premises: 'I have no money, but the money is in people's pockets.' Even though we are thousands of miles apart, our friendship hasn't been affected by distance and he is helping me with my new ministry for TV and radio streaming. Congratulations on publishing your book 'The FOG'. May it bring peace, joy and love around the world.'

Prof Samuel Tirtamihardja, owner of Tirta TV and Tirta radio, Indonesia

'But by the grace of God I am what I am, and His grace to me was not without effect.'
(1 Corinthians 15:10)
'Steve's love of Christ and passion to fulfil his calling to the nations with love, grace and service continues to impact lives. It was a true privilege to have served alongside Ps Steve and Ps Detty for many years.'

Pastor John and Pastor Judi Harwin, Living Word Lakeside Church, Australia

'You can feel the fullness of God's love permeating through the spirit of Pastor Steve Laidlow as he tells us how the Favour of God covers him throughout his ministry. May Christ be glorified through this book.'

Pastor Supeno Lembang, GKNS Agape Church, West Jakarta, Indonesia.

'This ordinary man has led an extraordinary life by stepping out and trusting God literally every step of the way. Our mission fields vary, and we do not always believe we are called to be missionaries unless we get on a plane. However, this book has reminded me that God can use all of us just where we are, as long as we put our hands in His and follow His lead, in faith.'

Kate Towers, Businesswoman and Centre Director of Tower Learning Centre Ltd, Blackpool.

'Do you want to live an extraordinary life? Beyond mediocrity? Look no further because this book will provoke destiny within you, inspire you to get out of your boat of comfort and ignite you to explore the life you were destined to live by the power of the Holy Spirit.
This book has further revealed the calibre of the man I've fallen madly in love with and now have the privilege of being married to!'

Pastor Ann Laidlow, Lead Pastor, Kings Church Blackpool

I dedicate this book firstly to God for
His faithfulness and favour over the years.
Secondly, I dedicate this book to my wife, Ann Laidlow, whom
God has brought into my life through His favour and Detty, my
late wife, who always supported, encouraged and faithfully
travelled with me all over the world until
she passed away in July 2016.
Thirdly, to our sons Greg and Thomas and family in England
and Germany who have been understanding and caring across
the miles and to our Indonesian daughters
who help and support us.
Last and not least, to all friends and family in every nation who
have helped to collate the contents of this book and to the
amazing Andi Robinson whose tireless editing, patience,
persistence and incredible focus to detail has made this
publication possible. Thank you for the countless hours you
have put in and to your team of proofreaders.
Thanks to all of you for believing in the ministry by prayerful,
financial and practical support. This has enabled me to fulfil
God's purpose and calling on my life in reaching the lost and
underprivileged people in South and South East Asia, making a
difference and helping them discover an extraordinary life.

ISBN 9781095699805
Imprint: Independently published

Contents

INTRODUCTION

'Let love and faithfulness never leave you; bind them around your neck, write them on the tablet of your heart. Then you will win favour and a good name in the sight of God and man.' (Proverbs 3:4)

If I'd have relied on logic and reasoning instead of trusting God and being led by the Holy Spirit, then I never would have got to this place in my life, let alone written a book about it! I would have said to God: 'No thank you. It's too much!'

I have told these stories of what God has done all over the world and so many people have said repeatedly, 'You should write a book.' And the time finally came to do something about it. So, read on!

'Let love and faithfulness never leave you; bind them around your neck, write them on the tablet of your heart. Then you will win favour and a good name in the sight of God and man.' (Proverbs 3:4)

For most of my Christian life, I have repeatedly heard the verses in the Bible that talked about how those who were devoted to the Lord would suffer persecution and criticism from others. I got the impression that I always had to choose between having God's favour or man's favour. However, once I started delving into the Scriptures, I realized that I could enjoy both.

The apostle Paul confirms this in Romans 14:18, saying, '*Anyone who serves Christ in this way is pleasing to God and approved by men.*' The truth is that if we just concentrate on pleasing God, He will give us favour with others when we need it most. We can even ask God to give us that favour. When we do that, we're not being selfish or prideful, but scriptural.

Nehemiah was an action man, a man of faith and a devoted servant of the Lord. He was called by God to rebuild the city walls of Jerusalem during the reign of King Artaxerxes. As cupbearer to the king, he asked the Lord to give him favour with the ruler so that he could complete his God-given assignment. '*Give Your servant success today by granting him favour in the presence of this man.*' (Nehemiah 1:11) Here, we learn an important Bible principle- that God will grant us favour with others when it will help us carry out His will, plans and purpose.

We can also pray for favour when we take a stand for the Lord. In the first chapter of the book of Daniel, the young prophet '*resolved not to defile himself with the royal food and wine,*' and he needed the co-operation of the chief official in order to carry out his commitment. Daniel 1:9 says, '*Now God had caused the official to show favour and sympathy to Daniel.*' When receiving favour will glorify God, we shouldn't hesitate to pray for it.

It's true that believers who are really committed to God will sometimes experience criticism and persecution. Jesus said we should count on it. He wanted us to know what we were getting into when we made the decision to follow Him. If we're making a difference for God, we can't expect Satan to just sit back and do nothing to try to hinder us. But the Bible teaches us that we can pray for God's favour, which can be a powerful weapon against the enemy's attacks.

We are God's children; His chosen; His elect. And He is committed to protecting and providing for His own. When we concentrate on pleasing God, we can depend on Him to change people's hearts for our benefit. Proverbs 16:7 says, *'When a man's ways are pleasing to the Lord, He makes even his enemies live at peace with him.'* If God is willing and able to change the hearts of our enemies, then we can expect Him to give us favour in the sight of our teachers, employers, neighbours and others we come in contact with.

Over the years, when my children have been treated unfairly at school by their teachers or fellow students, I have asked the Lord to give them favour and He has always been faithful. I have also asked God to grant my family favour in the sight of our bosses and co-workers. And I have seen my family acquire jobs that we were not even qualified for, often with salaries well above what we expected.

The grace of God is undeserved favour, which can be described as:

Faith
Activates
Victorious
Outrageous
Unlimited
Results

When you pray for favour, people will bless you, and they won't even know why. But don't just take my word for it. Begin today to pray for favour and discover for yourself that *'the Lord bestows favour and honour upon His people!'* (Psalm 84:11)

I've been praying for all members of the body of Christ to rise up, step out in faith, go places they've never been before and do things they've never done before. I believe this is the day God will speak to you. As you read this book, I believe the Holy Spirit will impart things to you, change the way you think and remind you of things He has already spoken to you about. I hope that you are going to catch something new, something fresh from God.

This is by no means a complete study in these areas, but rather an introduction to help you develop your faith, be led by the Spirit and help you discover how to live an extraordinary, victorious and effective Christian life.

Therefore, I encourage you to step out of your comfort zone by faith and discover the amazing plan God has for you!

Steve Laidlow

PART 1. THE FAVOUR OF GOD IN MY LIFE

1. HOW DID I GET HERE?

The Favour of God struck me in an amazing way while sat in the front row of a church on the other side of the world. The year was 2006 and I was in the Living Faith International Church that I had founded the previous year in Indonesia. I was enjoying a rare day off from preaching and our Associate Pastor, Bernie Berg, was at the front speaking and preaching about faith. About 15 minutes into the sermon, I felt so good and full of joy that I felt as if my feet were off the ground and I was floating above the chair. As I looked around at the congregation, I quietly asked: 'Lord, how did I get here? I'm just an ordinary guy from England, who left school with no qualifications, yet here I am running the show in South East Asia as the CEO of this ministry and Senior Pastor of this church! How did this happen?' The Lord answered: 'By faith. You've made a decision to trust me and step out of the boat.' It was an amazing, peaceful moment of coming to a realisation of everything that had happened since I gave my life to the Lord on March 9th, 1995 at the age of 43. My life was transformed and at a time when most people started thinking about retiring, I was re-firing!

It was a long way from where my life had started out. I was born on June 3rd, 1951 and was brought up by non-believing parents in Preston, North West England. I didn't believe in God, despite going through the traditional christening, confirmation and Holy

Communion ceremonies. In my mind it wasn't about God; it was about culture.

My aunt, Grace Moss, was a Christian and encouraged me to go to Sunday School. I stayed connected to the church when I became a Scout- it was just somewhere to go. But when I was 18, I discovered discos, bars and girls and left church behind, returning only for weddings, funerals and carol services.

What I do remember though, as a young adult, was the effect the Christmas Eve services had on me. I used to come out of the pub and into church to sing a few carols at Midnight Mass. I felt a connection with God and came out different somehow. And it wasn't the drink!

I'd left school at 15, did a six-year mechanical engineering apprenticeship and worked for United Kingdom Atomic Energy as a research and development engineer on power stations. I was promoted to technician, then supervisor then manager, and ended up as a company director. I remained in engineering for 35 years, until the age of 50.

I focused on my career and didn't give God much thought. However, but by the time I was in my 30's I developed an irrational fear of dying that came on me at work. When I went to the toilet, a claustrophobic feeling would come over me in the cubicle, thinking about dying and not being here or in control of my life. It scared me so much that I would run out as soon as possible. Sometimes I avoided going all day and waited until I got home because I didn't want that feeling to come. Looking back, I think even then the Holy Spirit was tapping me on the shoulder to get my attention. It was a good plan- or rather, a God plan!

I married my first girlfriend when I was 21. My dad tried to warn me against it, but at 21, I thought I knew what I was doing. Dads know best though. The marriage only lasted five years, despite having a son, Greg. I ended up divorced and back in the bars and discos, drinking, smoking and having a wild time.

I drifted along for quite a few years and then when I was 38, I took Greg on holiday to Spain. It didn't go too well; it took three days of the 10-day trip to get to a crummy hotel, with awful food, where it rained for three days! Once the rain stopped, we decided to walk along the beach and I spotted a nice-looking lady reading a book. I commented to her about the weather and she just stared at me looking confused. I soon realised that she didn't speak much English.

I moved to a sheltered café to light my cigarette away from the wind and saw her struggling to light hers. I sent Greg over to tell her to come to the café where it was less windy, and we got chatting. I found out that she was German and was called Detty.

A few days later, as we were getting to know each other, I said something that surprised me. We were sat round the hotel pool and these words came out of my mouth: 'God has brought us together for a purpose.'

Now, neither of us were Christians at this point. Detty came from a Catholic family of seven children, had also been married before and had a son, Thomas. We'd both said that we would never get married again, so I had no idea what I was saying or why. But even though we tend to think of God speaking to Christians in this way, He also has a plan for unbelievers' lives as well; that they are saved, filled with the Spirit of God and grow in order to be used for God's kingdom.

We started a long-distance relationship when I returned to England, travelling to each other's countries and spending lots of money on phone calls and letters. But one day we were at my brother-in-law's 40th birthday party and having a really good time. I was thinking how pretty she looked, with a pink waistcoat and a little pink ribbon in her hair. I suddenly decided to propose, and she said yes! We married in Preston registry office in May 1990 and set up home in Chorley, North West England.

Four years later, Detty went through a really difficult experience and at her lowest point, she cried out to God, saying: 'If You're the God and the Jesus that I heard about when I was a child, then You need to reveal yourself to me now and help me.' As she spoke, she felt a hand on her shoulder, heat go through her whole body and heard a voice said: 'It's going to be okay.'

Soon after that, she was invited to a Chinese cooking class by one of our neighbours. She was really excited when she came home and told me how friendly and joyful these ladies were and so different from anyone she had met before. They invited her to church at St John the Evangelist, Whittle-le-Woods and she became a regular attender and attended the Saints Alive course for new Christians.

She tried to tell me about it, but I wasn't interested. I was far away from God and would say things like: 'No way. This is like cult stuff from America. It's not the way you should be going, honey.'

About five months later, she asked me to pick her up from church one Sunday evening. It was an 18th Century Anglican church with thick oak doors that creaked open as I walked in. Inside there were about 30 people listening to the vicar, Don Gilkes, playing a guitar. I sneaked in and sat at the back. The vicar's wife, Dawn, came over to me.

'You must be Steve, Detty's husband,' she said.

I thought *how does she know me?* I found out later that Detty had been encouraged to ask me to pick her up so that I would meet some of these happy people. I was set up by God and the vicar's wife!

Dawn asked if I would like her husband to pray for me and I said rather dismissively: 'If he wants to. I mean if he's a bit bored and has nothing else to do.'

Don came over, laid hands on me and prayed. The next thing I remember was waking up on the floor, jammed between the pew and the kneeling pad. I was sweating and could hardly breathe. What on earth had just happened?

People came over and helped me up and sat me on the bench. I somehow recognised that it was an encounter with God. It opened my eyes and made me very inquisitive about Christianity.

I started attending the church and then was invited on the Saints Alive course. I took a friend along, Paul Harrison and on the 9th week, I was sat in the church with about 10 others, on hard, wooden pews in the freezing cold. I couldn't wait to give my life to Jesus!

A few before us had responded to the altar call and I elbowed Paul in the ribs and said: 'Are you ready for this?'
'I don't know about this. I'm not sure,' he responded. (His conversion came later and he became the church worship leader).

But I was ready. They called my name out from the front and I ran to the altar– I felt like I had running shoes on! I confessed Jesus as my Lord and asked Him to forgive all my sins. I fell to the floor again as I was baptised in the Holy Spirit and woke up speaking in tongues. I didn't even know what speaking in tongues meant!

That was on the 9th of March 1995 at 8:05 P.M. I was 43 years old. I'd turned from an unbeliever thinking this was a cult, to being on fire for God in nine weeks. It was an amazing experience and the best decision I've ever made.

Many years later, I preached at that church when I was on the mission field and Don and Dawn Gilkes, who are now retired, came to Indonesia and saw the result of their input into mine and Detty's lives. They helped to lay the foundation stone for the Acorn Centre. They cried every day at what they saw and couldn't believe that these two people whom they had introduced to God were doing all this and getting out of the boat!

A few days after I gave my life to Jesus, I was walking through the forest with our two Labrador dogs, Jason and Misty, when I suddenly raised my hands above my head and prayed: 'Lord, give me opportunities and situations to tell people about Jesus.' I'd never heard anyone say this before or read anything like this. It just came out. Our dogs, who were very well trained and used to hand signals, were looking at me as if to say: 'What kind of move is that? What do you want us to do?'

I didn't know at the time that I was speaking out 1John 5.14: '*This is the confidence we have in approaching God: that if we ask anything according to his will, he hears us.*' I just prayed with the faith of a newborn Christian, with the trust of a child. And God answered. Two weeks later, I was on a plane going to China with a suitcase full of Mandarin Bibles, with no idea that I was about to break the law!

Steve(centre) with his dad, Frank and son, Greg

2.HEART CRY FOR MISSION

My job as a research and development director involved regular international travel and three days after that prayer in the forest, myself and a colleague, Robin Hill, were asked by our managing director to go to China on engineering work for a couple of months. On hearing this, someone from church lent me the book, 'Heart Cry for China' by Ross Patterson. As I read it the Holy spirit inspired me to contact the number in the back of the book. I rang it straight away and asked how I could help Chinese Christians. I was told I would be sent a package.

The package arrived full of Mandarin Bibles, with some instructions that read: 'Please give this to the taxi driver and he'll tell you where the church is to take the Bibles to.' It felt like a James Bond mission! But I still had no idea that taking Bibles into China was illegal.

Once we arrived in China, I walked through customs with these 50 Bibles in my suitcase, obeying the Lord with complete peace of heart. I just smiled at the customs officer and walked through.

I had a 'poachers' waxed cotton jacket with lots of pockets inside to hide the Bibles. I handed some out in the street and saw the hunger and passion that people had for God's word. I then took the remaining 20 to the church indicated in the instructions. Underneath the church building was a police station.

I sat through the service and afterwards I told the pastor that I had some Bibles. He looked alarmed.

'You can't give them to me here,' he said.

'Can't you see all the guys around, guys in black suits and white shirts? They are monitoring what is going on in this church. You'll get me arrested.'

He told me to give them to a lady in the basement coffee shop, who hid them inside her bag. I found out that she was a teacher and wanted to use the Bibles to teach her students.

The contract work I was doing was in a factory in Bejing, with an interpreter called Jim. In my naivety I asked him if he was a Christian. He said nothing. They can get into serious trouble for admitting their faith and disappear or be persecuted.

After about three days he came to me and whispered: 'Yes I am a Christian.'

He told me that he didn't have a Bible and that his family had borrowed their uncle's copy for one day and everyone quickly hand-wrote scripture verses. That really touched my heart. I offered him a Bible and he came to collect it from my hotel room that night. As soon as I handed it over, his eyes looked like they were coming out on stalks, like in a cartoon! It was almost as if I'd given him a bar of gold.

Seeing the hunger and passion the Chinese Christians had for God's word proved to me how valuable it is in some countries. Some of us may have the luxury of having a number of different Bibles, but back then they hardly had any. And it's wonderful to think that some of those Christians could now be pastoring churches or reaching out in mission themselves.

Back at home, both Detty and I were baptised by full immersion in a private swimming pool because the Church of England didn't offer full immersion baptisms. We had the words from Isiah 61:3 spoken over us: 'They will be called oaks of righteousness, a planting of the Lord for the display of His splendour.' This became a landmark verse for our ministry and a confirmation in our spirit, but it would be another five years before we fully understood why.

I told our pastor, Don Gilkes, that I would like to help out in church. He said: 'Praise the Lord. We've been praying about a Fabric Manager.' I thought *wow, that seems like a pretty fancy title. Must be good benefits package or something.*

'We want you to take care of the gardens and graveyards, cut the grass and make everything presentable for people coming to church,' he said.

Not quite so fancy then! But I was faithful in that and looked after the gardens in all weathers. After about six months I asked if there was anything else I could help with. He asked me to be a greeter and an usher and help count the offering after the service. I said: 'Well, praise the Lord. So, who's going to cut the grass?'

'You are. That's an extra job.'

When we became Christians, we knew that our home would become a house for many others, especially children in need. One of the first girls we helped was an Italian lady called Alice, from Sardinia, Italy. She was studying at Runshaw College, where my wife was studying art. She was living with her Italian uncle, but her goal was to learn English. Detty suggested that she lived with us for a year. Now she's a media director of a British television channel.

Our burden for the lost and needy became greater and we opened our home to take in foster children, starting with three infant siblings who were rescued by the police and in need of shelter and care. It was tough and our marriage was tested. Only by God's grace did we survive. However, it was all worthwhile. The two older children have accepted Jesus in their hearts.

People at work had noticed the change in me. In fact, my sales manager told my divisional manager that I was taking drugs! When I asked him why he had said that, he explained that he had seen so much change in me. I didn't swear, I was courteous at meetings and I didn't tell dirty jokes as I had done on the shop floor. It was the only conclusion he could come to!

I actually got my line manager into my office and asked him to sit down. I said: 'I would like to ask forgiveness from you because I haven't treated you right as my manager and I've tried to show you up in meetings. And I'd like to tell you that I love you.'

He nearly fell off his seat! Tears came in his eyes. He couldn't believe what I was saying.

About six months after that I accepted voluntary redundancy after 23 years with United Kingdom Atomic Energy. It was a sign that God was starting to move me on in my new faith.

I got a job at Leisure Hall, Leyland, run by the Brothers of Charity for people with learning disabilities. I supervised teams in the garden, art room and hospital and helped with personal care (which would later come in very useful). I loved the work, but the pay was very poor.

About six months after this, I was headhunted by a cable company in Ashford, Kent, who were licensed to sell machines on behalf of United Kingdom Atomic Energy, my previous employer. We moved to Ashford and I became the research and development director. We then joined a local church, Ashford Christian Fellowship.

We still wanted to open our home to those in need and had two homeless alcoholics, Eddie and Stephen staying with us for about a month. We first met them when we were having an evangelistic mission. I was on the street encouraging people to go into our mission tent and these two men staggered by with carrier bags full of beer. I encouraged them to go in, where they gave their lives to Jesus.

A few days later, I came home from work and they were sat in the lounge cleaned up, shaven and wearing my clothes! I went into the kitchen to ask Detty what was going on. She said she'd seen them in town, brought them home, ran a bath for them, burned their clothes, gave them one my shavers and my clothes. And she wanted them to move into our spare room.

'Are you serious?' I said.

'Yes, I'm serious.'

'Sounds like a good plan,' I said.

We managed to find Eddie a job but I'm not sure what happened to Stephen after he left.

Our second mission trip came about when our pastor, Syd Doyle and his wife, Liz, were going to Kenya, Africa. We asked if we could join them and they agreed. We were excited. We thought we were going on holiday, but it seems that they had a different plan!

Once we got there, I was thrown in the deep end at an evangelistic crusade in a beer factory. I was helping to prepare by moving beer bottles out of the way and setting up the platform. Hundreds of people started to pour in, who were all singing and dancing.

Just as the crusade was starting, Syd said to me, 'Ok Steve, go on the platform now and speak.'

'Pardon,' I said, in surprise. 'You must be joking! I haven't prepared anything.'

He stuck the microphone in my hand as I protested, pushed me really hard and said: 'Get up there!'

Once on stage, all I could see in the dark was a sea of white eyes and teeth as the crowd waited for me to speak. They were probably thinking *what is this white guy going to say?* I was thinking *Lord, what am I going to say?*

I took a deep breath, brought the microphone to my mouth and yelled out: 'JESUS IS LORD!' It echoed across the beer factory. I was shocked. Where did that come from?

'YEEEESSS' they shouted back in excitement. I carried on preaching the gospel for 50 minutes and then there was an altar call, where people got healed and saved. One man came to the front still holding onto his bicycle because he didn't want to risk it being stolen. One of the African team looked after it for him.

I'd never experienced anything like that before. It was the start of my public ministry.

Another place we went to was like a huge, disused cinema, with lightbulbs hanging on wires. The place was full of about 500 people praising and worshipping God.

When we arrived there, the praise and worship came to a standstill. The African pastor got up and announced: 'We have some guests from England. Line up at the front here. They are going to pray for the sick.'

I'd never done this before and as they all stood in front of us, I silently prayed *Lord, help me. I don't know what to do.* But by faith, I laid hands on them and we saw amazing miracles before our eyes. I was just trusting God. I had no idea what I was doing, but He knew what He was doing! I'd never seen anything like that before and suddenly I'm there, seeing it for real. It made me want more opportunities like this.

Detty went to Tanzania to assist with a ladies' seminar and I went to Nairobi. We saw a lot of poverty, both financial and spiritual. You may think poverty is about people living on the streets, but billionaires can be very underprivileged because they've never heard the gospel.

That mission trip to Africa birthed a vision in mine and my wife's heart for underprivileged people.

Steve leading a Bible study

Travelling around Indonesia

3. SETTING THE CAPTIVES FREE

We returned to England and six months later we got connected with a Christian hairdresser called Cath, who worked in Southport. She was cutting hair for free at St Peter's Church, Birkdale to raise money for an orphanage project. The lady who normally helps her was ill. She was told about Detty, who was a trained hairdresser and got in touch to ask her to help.

We went together and found out that they were part of a charity helping to build orphanages in Timișoara, Romania. We joined as supporters and even offered to sell our house to donate money, but the director told us that this was foolish because we'd have nowhere to live! In addition, God wanted many people to be involved and not just one couple.

They were heading out six weeks later. We asked if we could join them and they agreed.

When we got there, we were shocked at the conditions. A lot of the buildings had bullet holes in them. The supermarkets had little more than a few loaves of bread on the shelves. It was so dark, grey and cold and the people were so depressed.

We went over twice, helping physically to build the playground and storehouse at the orphanage, but when we came back after the first trip, we went to the supermarket and both started crying. We couldn't believe that we had so much food and where we had come from had so little. It increased the burden in our hearts for underprivileged people.

We held fundraising events for the orphanages. We used to open our garden in England. Detty made cakes with cups of tea and I sold plants.

Cath was also instrumental in our first trip to India. She met a missionary, Ruel Morgan, at a conference in Manchester for underprivileged people. Ruel was born in the Caribbean, but ended up in Manchester, where he lived a wild life. He was given a five-year prison sentence, losing his son, his son's mother, his family, his job and his home. One day on the bunk bed in his cell, he cried out to God for forgiveness and got baptized in the Holy Spirit. He told me that it was like the whole bed was on fire around him.

At the conference, Ruel had already spotted Cath and before they had even spoken, he heard God tell him that she was going to be his wife. They got talking and pretty soon she was telling us that she was getting married in Bangalore, South India, where Ruel was on mission. Of course, we asked if we could come and they said yes.

We'd already agreed to do a bit of teaching there. However, when we got off the plane, we met Ruel for the first time and he gave us a full itinerary of preaching and teaching covering every day. And we thought we were going on holiday!

We were thrown in the deep end straight away and it was amazing. We visited unreached villages where they'd never heard about Jesus and we had opportunities to preach in many churches and teach many pastors.

At one crusade I gave an altar call for healing and two young dumb girls came up with their mother. Detty laid hands on the girls and they started speaking for the first time in their lives. Their mom, who was a Hindu, was so surprised and overjoyed that she was dancing and jumping around. She became a Christian straight away and we used her house to start a church, where we ran Bible studies.

We were all so busy with ministry, that we forgot about the big event. Ruel said to us one morning: 'What are we doing today?'

'Ruel, you're getting married!'

He'd forgotten and we had to rush out and get him a shirt from the market. Ruel's was black round the collar.

'You can't wear that Ruel. It's filthy,' I told him.

'But Bro, I'm getting married in two hours!'

We also had a Turkish shave and then the barber performed some chiropractor moves on us. I felt my neck click. Every bone in my back rattled! It loosened us up though.

Ruel also decided to have a facial, but the barber used body scrub on his face that rubbed his dark skin off. He came out of the shop white!

'Whoah,' said Cath when she saw him.

'Ruel, you've changed colour!'

We even went on honeymoon with them to Sri Lanka.

They both now live in Southport and Ruel still goes out on mission for three months at a time under his ministry and registered charity Work Spot. He also founded a school for around 350 children.

Over a period of about six years, we took many teams to India and fundraised in England, the USA and Singapore to buy equipment, such as generators, platforms, light and sound systems for evangelistic crusades. Sometimes at pastor's seminars, we taught in three different languages on subjects like faith, prayer and righteousness. We held crusades every night in different places, with teams often travelling for six hours. At one seminar, there were 350 pastors and we took turns to teach for 12 hours a day over five days. We were so hoarse that we could barely speak.

We also helped to plant 25 churches and helped Rays of Peace ministry to build an orphanage for 35 children.

Another mission under Rays of Peace resulted in a threatening situation that God used for His glory. We had planned a three-night crusade in one village and on the first night, the villagers were very offended by what we were saying. Some had guns and threatened to burn down the whole platform with us on it and beat us openly. We also saw someone pointing a gun at us from behind the trees, which we only spotted when we turned on the van's headlights. He immediately ran away.

We left that night, but in the van, the ministry's senior pastor Mark Jayakumar suggested going back with gifts and inviting the troublemakers onto the platform as VIP's. So, we wrapped Bibles up for them and handed them out the next night. The whole village got saved, including those who had threatened us!

One of our mission trips to Bangalore lasted 10 days, travelling more than 2,000 miles with a team of 16 people from six countries. We ran teaching seminars, crusades, youth, children's and women's ministries. Altogether we ministered to 7,400 people, had 1,890 salvations, 1,200 people baptized in the Holy Spirit and 2,700 healings- many of them instant.

One of the miracles was a blind lady that the whole crowd knew. She was led forward and a young Vietnamese lady, Rebecca, who I went to Bible school with, joined me. I told her: 'Lay hands on her. Use the power.' As soon as she did, this lady's eyes opened, and her sight was restored! Oh, I tell you she was full of joy- singing, dancing, running around, seeing things that she'd never seen before. We couldn't contain her!

Another one was a crippled man with a shrivelled arm, who came limping forward at the altar call. His leg was twisted around a stick and as I laid hands on him the power of God entered his body, the stick dropped to the floor, his leg became straight, his shrivelled arm was straightened out and he started jumping up and down saying 'hallelujah' and praising God.

At the end of one crusade, I was asked to pray for an Indian lady who had been in a wheelchair for 16 years. I left the platform praying: 'Lord, you've got to help me now.' Despite seeing many miracles, this was challenging because it stretched my faith. But when you realise that you are just a vessel for God to do His work, you have confidence in His power. So, in boldness, I laid hands on this lady and she jumped out of the wheelchair and started running around the crusade ground!

Praying in confidence can change many situations. A friend in India, Terri Johns, went to her garage to pick up a stick that she used to drive cattle out of the garden. As she reached over, a huge king cobra raised up in front of her and hissed. She had an opportunity to run away but she didn't. She said, 'In the name of Jesus get out of here!' It sank down and slithered out of the garage!

You see, when you put your faith into action, you will see things that you could never dream of or imagine. But I also think that we've seen such powerful moves of God in Asia because people have lived in the spiritual world for so long already– white magic, black magic and eastern religions. They already have the discipline of fasting and getting up early to pray and to read the Scripture. Just by changing who they worship they see the changes in their life. They are more willing to believe than others in a more secular society. They experience miracles and they are spectacular. They see the change and they want it.

But being open to spirituality means that they can be bowing down to demonic spirits without realising and can become demon possessed.

The first time I experienced this, it was pretty scary. I was working with Rays of Peace ministry with pastor Mark Jayakumar and his wife, Francina. We attended a TB hospital in India for about 200 women. They were the worst conditions I have ever seen– the bed sheets were filthy, there was dirt everywhere, the furniture was broken and there were cats wandering around the wards.

I went round with two interpreters, giving each patient a bread roll, a banana and a tract, provided by a local pastor. We also prayed for people and after I prayed for one lady, the Holy Spirit said: 'Go and pray for that lady again.'

The interpreters were protesting because I'd already prayed for her, but I knew I needed to be obedient. As soon as I laid hands on her, a demon manifested in her and she became like an animal, writhing and twisting and levitated off the bed, like there was a magician there. People were trying to hold her arms and legs and I said: 'In the name of Jesus, you foul spirit, come out of her,' while I was thinking *Lord, help me! I don't know what to do.*

There was such a commotion going on that Detty and Sister Francina came running down the ward. By this time there was a crowd of people around the bed, including patients, all watching. I hadn't been to Bible school at this point, but I'd read the Bible, so I used my authority in the name of Jesus. Suddenly, the lady collapsed on the bed, opened her eyes and smiled. The demon had gone.

We cleaned her up and led her to Jesus. It was amazing. She turned out to be really pretty, but she didn't look like that when she was being overtaken by this demon spirit.

We'd promised her a Bible in her language, which we took to her the next day. As we arrived, she came running down the ward with a clean dress on. She'd showered and washed her hair, which was flowing out behind her as she ran. We gave her the Bible and she was so thankful and so happy.

We had planned to go to a cancer hospital in Bangalore to lay hands on the sick, but as we walked away, Francina said: 'It reminds me of Jesus' time Brother Steve.'

'What do you mean Sister Francina?'

'Just look behind us.'

As I looked, there was a crowd of people following us, who had got out of their beds.

'What can we do for you?' I asked.

'Can you pray for us like you prayed for the lady yesterday?'

You see, they saw something happen in the spiritual realm. They saw her set free and saw the change in her life.

On another Indian crusade, someone manifested a spirit when I was preaching. He was like a spinning top, twirling around on the floor and then started acting like a snake, moving through the crowd. The devil always tries to attract attention and disrupt things. I wasn't distracted and just carried on.

He came forward when I gave the altar call and it turned out that he was the priest of two Hindu temples. He had long dreadlocks, fingernails and toenails that were long and curled, and covered in absolute filth that you could almost scrape off his body. But he gave his life to Jesus.

The next night, one of the pastors said to me: 'See the guy on the drums. That's the Hindu priest from last night.' He'd had a haircut, shave and was wearing clean clothes. He looked really happy. He agreed to give his testimony and told everyone: 'I encourage all you people here to go to the new church that's starting in this village.'

A few years later, when we were in Indonesia, a church member came to me after the morning service and said: 'My sister is demon-possessed. Can I bring her to you today and you can cast that demon out of her?'

My first thought was *why don't you do that?* I always tell people that they have the same power, the same word, the same Jesus that I have, but sometimes people think that church leaders are the only ones who have the power!

But then I'm always willing, so I agreed and called a couple of friends to assist. One of them, John Harwin, was a strong, muscular Australian rugby player.

We all gathered in my office, sat down and I said to this lady: 'So, what's happening?' Suddenly she turned into this lion, with hands like claws and she came for my throat. I grabbed her by the wrists, swung around and dropped her into John Harwin's lap. She was such a tiny lady, but suddenly she had the power of 10 men and we all ended up wrestling with her on the floor as she dragged us around. Then she tried to get out under a gap in the door like a snake. But after several minutes, that demonic spirit came out of her and she gave her life to Jesus.

You need to remember as a minister to keep your eyes open because someone might just smack you when manifesting! That's happened several times and I've ended up scratched and dripping blood.

In circumstances like this, never miss an opportunity to lead somebody to Jesus, even though it might be the first time you've dealt with demons. Jesus dealt with them very quickly. I'm talking about using your authority in the name of Jesus. He overcame the works of the devil. Speaking that out with power and authority and the devil has to leave. He cannot stand it.

Jesus said in Mark 16:17-18: '*In My name they will cast out demons; they will speak with new tongues; they will take up serpents; and if they drink anything deadly, it will by no means hurt them; they will lay hands on the sick, and they will recover.*'

There are a lot of demons out there in the world, but when we know the power and authority in the name of Jesus, we have nothing to fear.

Another place we got involved in was Thailand, where I travelled to regularly on business trips. Through friends we met Pastor Luke and his wife, Tutu, in Chiang Mai. Tutu was from the Karen Long Neck Tribe and wore the traditional tribal dress. She had a real heart for helping girls escape the thriving sex trade there.

It was common for parents to sell their daughters– some as young as 14– to work as prostitutes in the cities. The girls would send money home to support the parents and the villages. It's hard for us to imagine what it's like for these parents to be so desperate financially, that they would be willing to do that, but it was a way of keeping themselves alive. When people are in survival mode, selling their bodies is just one of many things they feel they must do.

We helped set up a hostel for about 20 girls, who received food, clothing, education and training, such as hairdressing and sewing, so that they could get work other than prostitution. The work is still thriving today.

We travelled to many bamboo church buildings and slept in bamboo huts on stilts to stop snakes coming up in the night. Pastor Luke translated for me, even though his English wasn't too good. My friend, Ruel, came with us and sometimes preached.

Those early mission experiences changed my life and I recognised more and more God's plan and calling. But God had bigger plans for us. Life was about to change again.

4.TRAINING FOR THE HARVEST FIELD

In 2001, at 3am God spoke to me in a booming voice– an early morning wake up call.

'Steve, get more training to be more effective in My harvest field.' That was it. No other instructions. I looked around the bedroom. I looked at Detty and thought *she hasn't got a deep voice like that. It must be God.*

I didn't want to disturb her, so I went downstairs and debated with God for several hours: 'Lord I can't really believe what I'm hearing here. We've been going overseas. We've spent all our money and our time. We've taken holidays without pay. We've seen many people saved. We've seen the blind eyes open. We've seen the dumb speaking. We've seen the lame walking and you're telling me we need to get more training to be more effective! Are you sure Lord?'

'Yes,' he said.

There was no doubt about it then. I knew for sure that God wanted me in full-time ministry. I had to tell my wife. I ran upstairs to wake her.

'Detty, Detty, you'll never believe it. God just spoke to me!'

'Praise the Lord,' she muttered, sleepily.

Since Detty was a gregarious and assertive German, I was surprised at her brief response.

'Is that it? Is that all you can say? God just spoke to me about our future! Don't you understand?'

She then explained that God had already spoken to her three years earlier about the same thing. Since then she had been praying for God to tell me!

At the time I was enjoying a successful career, with a good salary, a company car, first-class international travel and a company credit card for expenses. We had a lovely big house in Kent, with a large garden. It was a great life.

Detty also had her own profession. She managed a home for single parents, run by the Methodist church. Now things would change for us both. But it was so easy, because we knew it was God. We wrote our resignation letters the next day.

I believe that God inspired me to write my resignation letter to my managing director, explaining my call to full-time ministry and my requests, which were to work part-time as a consultant and for the company to pay for mine and Detty's travel if we went to India and Thailand on mission (I offered to forfeit my usual first class travel so that Detty could come with me in economy).

As I handed it to my managing director and owner of the company, he read it, looked up at me from his big leather office chair and said: 'The first thing that comes to mind, Steve, are clouds and cuckoo land! I don't believe that anybody has got a higher calling on you than I do.'

Trying not to offend him, I smiled and replied: 'I believe you're wrong. I've heard from God. I believe He's calling me to Bible school.'

I didn't hear anything for three months. Finally, about five minutes before quitting time on the day before Detty and I were heading to India for six weeks, my boss told me that I'd got everything I'd asked for in my resignation letter.

We did our research and requested information from many Bible colleges worldwide and applied to Kingdom Faith Bible College in Southern England (now Kingdom Faith Training College). We got accepted, but God had other plans.

On a visit to our friends Cath and Ruel Morgan, we spotted a magazine on the beside cabinet called Word of Faith, talking about mission work. It was by Rhema Bible Training College and I became curious. I found out that there was one in Bangkok, Thailand, where I did consultancy work. We applied and attended an interview with the dean, Gary Crowl, on our next trip out. He explained that we would only get half the training because it was delivered in Thai and it would take up training time to translate to English. He then told us that a new RBTC was starting in Singapore in August that year. We didn't even know where Singapore was! But we knew it would be more suitable because training was delivered in English– Singapore used to be a British colony.

We left Thailand with application forms and travelled to India on mission. While we were there, God told us very clearly to fill them in and send them, so we found a telephone and fax shop– a common service in India for calling overseas. We faxed them to Rhema's Singapore office.

While travelling back from that mission trip, we were celebrating our 11th wedding anniversary. We had the choice of visiting Singapore to check out the facilities at the new college or to laze around in a beautiful hotel in Thailand. We chose Singapore and the next day pastor Yew Kwong, one of the instructors, showed us around the college facilities. We also attended Faith Family Church that was attached to the college.

On arriving back in England, we opened an email to say that we had both been accepted. It was amazing. We were so excited.

Further confirmation came when we sold our house in preparation for our time at Bible college. We'd previously rented and were debt and mortgage free. God told us to buy a house, even though we were reluctant to take on another mortgage. But we obeyed and 18 months later when we were accepted to Bible college, we put the house on the market. Within a few days we had three offers for the asking price! We ended up choosing a Christian couple and I sold the garden contents like the greenhouse and shed on top of that.

Because of the rise in house prices, we made £65,000 on the sale- enough to provide for us while at Bible college for two years! We then understood why God had told us to buy a house. He had everything covered.

We bought a smaller, maintenance-free flat, in Ashford, Kent, but we never lived in it, even though we ended up owning it for 17 years. We rented it out and it paid for us on the mission field after Bible college. All in God's plan. When it's God's plan, he pays. When it's our plan, we pay.

There was one more thing in God's plan that we needed to do before leaving the UK. Back in 1998 we were doing an evangelistic event in Canterbury and a lady asked us what the name of our ministry was. I didn't know what she was talking about, I was so naïve. Suddenly she said: 'The name of your ministry is Acorn. And she said the scripture is Isiah 61.3: 'They will be called oaks of righteousness, a planting of the Lord for the display of His splendour.' These were the same words we'd had spoken over us at our baptism!

Two years later, I was on an Indian crusade and the Lord spoke again, saying: 'Steve, now is the time to start your ministry.' I started writing down ideas, even though I had no idea how I was going to go about this. In 2001, we returned to India on a four-week mission. On January 20th, we were in Bangalore and I was about to preach at a crusade. As I was preparing and praying, the Lord revealed to me to set up a UK-based charity and pioneering ministry to win people, build people and send people through evangelism, study and mission training. He talked to us about a structure, website and business cards. I'd not thought about setting up a proper charity before that and certainly not 30 minutes before I was about to preach at a crusade!

In addition to preparing to leave for Bible college, we officially set up Acorn International Ministries in Preston as a registered charity. I even put Indonesia in the original application before it was even on the radar!

We didn't do any research into Singapore before going, not even to find out the currency. We just stepped out by faith, gave our possessions away and left England on July 19th, 2001. Yet I recall having more peace than I ever had in my life! It was like somebody had removed all the burdens of everyday life. We'd given both of our cars away, along with furniture, the freezer and the washing machine. We even gave our dog away! We were leaving everything behind and it was a new beginning. All we had were two suitcases, a backpack each and our tickets to Singapore. We had no idea what was going to happen. It was a beautiful feeling. It's one I recommend that you experience by faith in God and being led by the Holy Spirit.

Once we arrived in Singapore, we settled into the Family Faith Church and during one prayer time, I had a vision. It was like I was looking down on Singapore and there was a rainbow over the whole island. It was squeezing in at both sides and as it squeezed, light, arrows and sparks were shooting out. The Lord reminded me of two scriptures: Matthew 9:37-38, *'Then he said to his disciples, "The harvest is plentiful, but the workers are few. Ask the Lord of the harvest, therefore, to send out workers into his harvest field,"'* and also Malachi 4:2, *'But for you who revere my name, the sun of righteousness will rise with healing in its rays. And you will go out and frolic like well-fed calves.'* I believe God was referring to the missionaries going out from Singapore. This city was the hub to reach Asia with the gospel.

One week later during another house group prayer meeting, I had the same vision. But this time, money was dropping from the centre of the rainbow all over Singapore.

I recognized that Singapore is ideally positioned to reach out to South and South East Asia, where nearly half the world's population live. I knew that we had made the right decision to train there.

Bible college was fantastic. The spiritual growth was amazing and we learned so much. And the added bonus of having funds to support us meant that we didn't have to fit in jobs around our studies and had time to type up our notes, which I'm still using in teaching to this day!

God didn't just teach us from His word, he also taught us through our experiences, particularly around money. One afternoon after a class about praying in faith, Detty said: 'The orphanage in India needs £1,000, so we're going to pray for it to come into our ministry so we can bless them with it.'

'Wow, you've got more faith than I have!' I wasn't 100% trusting God for £1,000 back then. So Detty prayed a very simple prayer, no crying, screaming or crawling on the floor! We forgot about it and didn't write it down.

Six months later we were in England and a Chinese couple, who are friends of ours came to visit. They started talking about India and as they left, they handed me an envelope.

'What is this?'

'It's some money for the kids in India,' I was told.

We had not told them anything about our prayer six months previously and when they left, we counted the money. It was £1,000! It was given to the orphanage right at the point of their need, praise God! His timing is always perfect.

The legacy lives on and even after all these years, some of the children who grew up there still message me; many of them are pastors in various villages.

The Bible school was held at Paya Laber Methodist Church. It was their 75th anniversary and they had one million Singapore dollars to give away to mission organizations. They wanted to give some to our newly-formed Acorn charity.

'Could you come tomorrow and meet the pastor and the mission director, bring along your brochures and other things and then we can see how we can support you,' we were told. The only problem was, we didn't have any brochures. We hadn't written anything down at this point.

That evening I stayed up all night putting together our first brochure on our computer. It had a horrible, fuzzy photograph on the front and I only printed out two copies, but it helped me focus on what God was calling us to do.

Living in Singapore felt almost like living in England because we only went to college and church. We weren't tourists and knew little about the area. In fact, after being there for six months, my sister, Janet Brown, came to visit us and she asked us about places to go. I had no idea. In the end, we saw more in 10 days with my sister than we did for the whole year that we were there! But that time was so valuable, and it was one of the best times in my life.

We continued with short-term missions while at Bible college and one of them was in Vietnam. During our Christmas break, we went to Ho Chi Minh City, where we met some underground pastors. Because it's a communist country, churches are monitored by the government. The pastor must take his preaching notes to the police station before the Sunday service and they were checked to make sure he wasn't speaking out against the government. An official attended the service to monitor it. They are very strict; one pastor got a knock on the door five minutes after going on the internet and was asked by officials why he was on a Christian website.

We got introduced to an old pastor in his 80's who had been arrested many times for preaching the gospel. He showed us his bedroom and behind the door was a curtain covering a bookcase with all his sermons in.

Out of the 35 students at RBTC Singapore, we were the only foreign ones, but we made some good friends who I'm still in touch with today. The only other English-speaking person was the dean, Gary Crowl. We got to know him and after a year he was called back to the main campus in Oklahoma. He'd told us a lot about America and we saw it as a chance to meet with different groups of people, so we asked if we could come with him. His response was that he didn't know because he'd never been asked that question before!

In the end, we were given permission to complete our second year in Oklahoma from August 2002. It was very different to Singapore; there were 1,000 pupils instead of 35 and everything is so big in America. We also had RBTC founder Kenneth Hagin senior as one of our tutors.

We ended up getting a big 5-litre Cadillac because we thought we'd never have another chance to drive one. It was a massive custom cruiser that could fit four people in the front and could be used as a sleeper in the back. It was like driving a boat, it was so comfortable. However, we had to plan our journeys by petrol stations because it used so much fuel!

In our second year we had a choice of study options: evangelism, worship, mission or the pastor's course. We'd done mission and evangelism and we couldn't sing, so we chose the pastor's course! It was fantastic.

We met groups of people called to the same mission areas as us. Detty and I joined two other ladies in prayer every Tuesday evening and for about 95 % of the time, we prayed in the Spirit about reaching Asia. I had no idea I would be going to Indonesia. I was just praying along with the prayer group.

Graduating in 2003 was very spectacular. There were 600 of us in red gowns and hats, with white sashes. We were surrounded by flags representing the countries of the graduates and Kenneth Hagin Senior spiritually passed the baton to us and sent us out into the mission field. I was ordained as a Minister of the Gospel and here I was at the age of 52, not winding down but winding up! Instead of retiring, I was re-firing!

Kenneth Hagin Snr 'passing the baton'

5. INDONESIA

Before we graduated, we were attending a healing meeting, when the guest speaker said: 'There are some people in this room who have been ordained to go to Indonesia.' At another meeting, someone else said: 'I've just seen legions of angels going to Indonesia to prepare the ground.' These messages kept coming and eventually Detty and I went to speak to Gary Crowl about it.

'Praise the Lord', he said. I'd had a similar response from Detty when God told me to get more training.

'Why did you say that?'

'Because RBTC Indonesia is in the process of starting a program. It might be good for you to contact the directors to see if you can be of assistance to them.'

We were coming to the end of Bible school and we suddenly found ourselves being invited to help pioneer a new one in the largest Muslim nation in the world! There was no salary or house or anything. In fact, we didn't even know where Indonesia was and had to look it up on the map!

As much as we were excited, it was difficult to leave our two grown-up sons and elderly parents back in England. My dad said: 'You've got to do what you've got to do,' even though he wasn't a Christian at this point. Our sons released us, but we could sense that they couldn't really understand why we were going so far away.

It was hard, but as God's Word tells us, '*everyone who has left houses or brothers or sisters or father or mother or wife or children or fields for my sake will receive a hundred times as much and will inherit eternal life*'

(Matthew 19:29). We have experienced this and now have so many people all over the world who are our universal family.

God wanted us to put everything behind us and completely rely on Him. I was still working as a part-time consultant and on the way to Indonesia we stopped at Thailand so I could complete a 10-day consultancy project. On the final day, about 10 minutes before we were leaving, we had a message from the technical director of the company in England saying that because the company wasn't doing too well, they could no longer keep me on as a consultant.

'Oh hallelujah' I said. That was the end of the salary. We were now full-time faith missionaries!

We found out later that on the same day, Kenneth Hagin Senior, the founder of RBTC had gone home to be with the Lord. He truly had passed the spiritual baton onto us.

We arrived in Indonesia with only two bags and a backpack. We stayed with the only person we knew, Hendrik Chandra- his wife attended RBTC with us. We hadn't been there long when we heard a bomb go off in the Marriott Hotel just behind us. Can you imagine? We've gone on the mission field with our two bags and said: 'Here we are Lord! We've arrived.' And then, BOOM!

Indonesia is the fourth largest nation in the world. It's made up of 18,000 islands, only 6,000 of which are occupied. Some islands still have cannibals.

In 2003, it had a population of 252 million people in 300 ethnic groups. There are 37 million people living in poverty, 30 million people unemployed, 27% of babies lack nutrition and 36 million lack food. More than 5 million children can't continue with their education. Most Indonesian families live off less than two dollars a day.

It is the largest Islamic nation in the world, with 87% Muslim and they have the largest mosque in Southeast Asia. There is a small percentage of Hindus and Buddhists and only 6% Christian- as little as 1% in some places.

Friday was their day of prayer and it was a nightmare. There were traffic jams, nowhere to park and everything finished at lunchtime, when they would get their mats out in the streets. Droves of people went to the mosques. I'm not sure how much they understood because it was all preached in Arabic.

I went in a couple of mosques to understand how they worshipped. They were noisy places and everyone was bowing down with their heads on the floor. I believe that the Muslim faith is one of fear and control. They do it because they have to.

RBTC was going to be set up in Jakarta, the Indonesian capital, with a population of 17 million. It's noisy, smoky, with endless traffic jams and a great divide between rich and poor. There are rules, but Indonesian people don't like obeying them. They drive through red traffic lights. If you try to walk on the pedestrian crossing, they go around you with motorbikes.

We had a lot to learn about the language and culture, so we attended IMLAC (Inter Missions Language Acquisition Centre) in the hills of Bandung, which is a four-hour drive from Jakarta.

There were about 20 students at IMLAC, but we were taught one to one. On the first day the teachers spoke perfect English to introduce themselves and orient us to the place, but after that they never spoke another word of English.

We had to learn Indonesian intensively for four hours every morning and in the afternoon, we had to go out and interview 15 people. The next day we had to report our findings to the whole class in Indonesian.

It was very tough. It was a hard language and my hard drive was already full! I'd been an engineer for 35 years and suddenly, at the age of 53, I was learning a new language. I kept laughing my head off at how strange it all was. I was still trying to learn English!

We lived in the local Kampung (shanty town) in a tiny, damp, one up one down house on the side of a hill. It had one tap, one gas jet and 900w of electricity. We couldn't even boil a 2kw kettle. If Detty tried to put a hairdryer on, it tripped the switch.

There were mosques all around us and every morning, at 4am, there was a call to prayer over loudspeakers. I often joked that I would re-connect the wires to play praise and worship music instead!

The temperature was very uncomfortable. It was about 30°C, with a humidity of 95%, so you are constantly sweating whenever you step outside the buildings. The food is hot and spicy and Indonesians eat rice at least three times a day.

We didn't have a car for the first nine months and travelled everywhere on little minibuses called angkots, carrying shopping bags for miles.

One day, I came back from shopping and saw Detty sat outside the house crying.

'What's the matter?' I was concerned.

'I've just had a vision,' she said.

'I've just seen people walking past our house, but I've seen them going to hell.' God was speaking love and compassion through her and it spurred us on even more to reach the lost.

But after two months, there was a moment when it all became too much and I nearly gave in. I came back to the house with a steaming headache. I've had otosclerosis (hearing loss) since the age of 25, which made everything more difficult at the language learning centre. I was living in this poky, damp place with no transport and no luxuries. We'd given everything up, to live with Muslims in a foreign country and we were having a hard time.

I lay on the bed and said to Detty: 'What on earth are we doing here? Why are we going through all this? Where are the suitcases?'

'I have my hand on them under the bed. Should I get them out?'

'Put them away,' I said. 'I'm only speaking in the flesh and not by the Spirit. We'll get over this. 'It was the only time in all our years on the mission field that I have ever had those doubts.

Our time in that tiny house was also the only time I had ever felt fear in Indonesia. The local security 'Mafia' operated in the area, who demanded money from people for so-called protection. They wandered around at night with leather jackets, signalling to each other by banging on steel lampposts, like some kind of Morse code. Once it woke me up in the middle of the night and startled me and I felt a bit of fear in that moment. I got over it by going back to sleep!

But, despite the dangers of earthquakes, mudslides, tsunamis, Christian persecution and jihad training groups, Indonesia felt like the safest place we'd ever lived in. We even felt safer than Preston town centre on a Friday evening! We were in God's will and had nothing to be afraid of.

We'd had many confirmations from God about Indonesia; one was the symbol of the eagle. We didn't put two and two together until we arrived there.

When I first met Detty on the beach in southern Spain, she was reading a book called 'The Eagle has Landed' and then when we were at Bible school in Oklahoma, I was in our weekly prayer group and I got a vision of an eagle hovering above a fire in a forest. Every time the eagle flapped its wings, the fire spread out. When I told the others, they said: 'Praise the Lord, America is going to be part of this.' The eagle is the emblem of America. Then when we arrived in Indonesia nine months later, we walked into a little Presbyterian church and behind the vicar was a huge eagle on the wall. It turns out that it's the logo for Indonesia. An eagle is also on all the coins.

When we returned from Bandung to Jakarta, we rented a large, beautiful house for very little money through a friend and started setting up the new Bible school. We had to prepare plans and lectures and teach six subjects. It was hard for us, but after two years, we graduated the first class of about 35 Indonesian students.

We've seen real fruit from this over the years and one student is a worship leader at a church with 3,000 and he is teaching praise and worship at the Bible school. Others are pastoring churches or teaching.

We also started attending a nearby church, International Full Gospel Fellowship (IFGF). On the first Sunday that we attended, a Pilipino tapped me on the shoulder and asked if I would be interested in helping to start an English-speaking branch of the church. We said no. We had come to reach Indonesian people. However, we were persuaded to attend a meeting about it and by the time we came out, I was the pastor and evangelist and Detty was in charge of the children's church!

I was in that role for about a year and during that time they had a new backcloth made. I didn't have anything do to with the design. It turned out to have an eagle on it!

It was at this church that we met Noel and Rose Trinder. They walked in halfway through the service and sat on the front row. After they left, I said to Detty that we needed to watch them because they were very special people. That could only have been a word of knowledge, because I had no idea who they were. They became an important part of our work and good friends over the years.

In addition to this role, I was teaching at the Bible school for five mornings a week and helping to plant churches in India, Pakistan and the Philippines as the church's representative in Asia.

Pakistan stands out in my mind. I worked with Pastor Saleem Bashir running an open-air crusade. and because I used to volunteer as a special constable in the Lancashire Constabulary police force, I was sent out by the IFGF to check security for the event. There's a lot of Christian persecution in Pakistan, which is mostly a Muslim country.

Once the crusade started, there were police officers outside with machine guns guarding us and then I came face to face with the tallest guy I've ever seen in my life, holding a big gun. Pastor Saleem told me it was his best church member who had brought his best gun to protect us.

He marched us down the aisle to the platform in front of a huge crowd and on nearby roofs were the silhouettes of men with machine guns. We preached the gospel, people got saved and healed and then we left with our 'bodyguard', jumped into the back of the taxi and drove back to reality. We'd stepped into the spiritual, supernatural realm during the crusade and then back to the natural realm, almost like Dr Who travelling from one time zone to another!

In addition to our church and bible school ministry in Indonesia, we both served at Springfield International School that sponsors missionaries to teach there. It is a Christian school and students from Buddhist and Muslim families heard the gospel. I was the Friday pastor and Detty taught there, eventually becoming the principal.

Many students accepted Christ in Detty's classroom. The kids were so beautiful. They often said to her: 'We love you Miss Detty,' and it brought tears to her eyes. Detty's calling was children's ministry and she loved it.

After surviving without a car for nine months, Hendrik Chandra blessed us with an eight-seater Kia Carnival a week before a mission team arrived from England and America. Later, Noel and Rose Trinder blessed us with a new Suzuki as well. The registration number on the license plate on one car was OM. We called it 'Operation Mobilization' and we decided to use it for the food distribution after the flood in 2009.

Not long after getting our Kia car, a Muslim man called Pak Taufik approached me, offered to be our driver and handed us his CV. We took him on and he drove us to all our church meetings. He used to sit at the back of the church listening to the teaching. One day he came to me and said: 'I've got good news for you, pastor. I'm now a born-again Christian.' I thought that I would have the privilege of leading him to the Lord, but he went with a friend to a church and he and his wife responded to the alter call. He changed his Muslim name from Taufik to Victor. He became a great evangelist and led his auntie, his grandma and a Muslim friend to Jesus! Speaking of his friend, he said in excitement: 'I was so shocked, because Scriptures just came out of my mouth.'

He was our driver for nine years and became a student at Rhema Bible Training Centre, in Lippo Karawaci , West Jakarta.

6. BACK TO THE VISION

Everything seemed to be going well. But one day the Lord said to me: 'Steve, what are you doing?' I was confused.

'What do you mean? We're doing all of this stuff for you.'

'This is not what I called you to do,' He told me.

'This is the IFGF vision, but I want you to follow the vision I've given you.'

That's when He asked us to step out in faith, which led to the launch of Acorn Indonesia in 2005 (legally, churches in Indonesia have to come under a charity). The new charity, like Acorn International Ministries, consisted of three separate arms: Living Faith International Church, Word of Faith Bible School and Seeds of Faith Humanitarian.

Living Faith International Church started in our house with 12 people. When that got too small, we moved to Noel and Rose Trinder's house. Six months later, that was too small, so we decided to rent space in a building owned by Heartline Radio. The station was part of Far Eastern Broadcasting Corporation- a Christian organisation that plants radio stations around the world to get the message of the gospel out to Muslim areas. Professor Samuel Tirtamihardja, who is still one of my best friends, was the founder.

I visited the new building initially with Noel, one of our trustees and Professor Tirtamihardja showed us this vast empty space with a ceramic tiled floor.

'How much do you need?' he said.

'All of it,' I replied.

'All of it?' He was rather surprised. It was huge.

I signed a five-year contract for the space with zero money in the bank. And, of course, the money came through!

Some believe that money to fund Acorn Indonesia came from people in highly developed nations like America or Europe. But most of the funding came from people God brought into our ministry. Heads of companies and schools came in to be our trustees and we had a lot of CEO's and top businessmen attending. The money was certainly in Indonesia and God made sure that it was released to support the ministry.

When Detty and I started the Living Faith church, I felt like a conductor of an orchestra. Everything just came together- the people, finances and resources were in place as God provided everything needed to build His church. We didn't worry about where the money was going to come from. But when you're following God's plan for your life and have faith, you can have complete peace, knowing that He will provide.

Once it was set up, we had an amazing facility that could fit 500 people for the service. We also had a second service for Indonesian people.

We took the opportunity to use Heartline Radio to spread the gospel and hosted a weekly radio show every Sunday evening. Listeners could call in with questions or prayer requests after we had preached the gospel and had Bible teaching. We ran this for nearly eight years and had an audience of six million. It was a powerful ministry and even though many didn't have television in Indonesia, most people had radios. We had a good response and testimonies from listeners were plentiful.

I remember one chap asking me to pray for his wife's asthma and for him to stop smoking. I said I guess we just need to pray for you because if you don't smoke, her asthma will be better!

Once, a friend from the leprosy community gave his testimony and people called in for prayer for healing, because he was so powerful. He was the strongest man spiritually I've ever known in my life, even though his body was wasting away.

We also started doing seminars for the listeners on Saturdays, so that we could answer their questions in person.

Another opportunity came through an organisation called TV 21, part of Televillage, a mobile video library. We worked in the studio with translators, then the van drove round villages with the teaching tapes and lent them to villagers. It was another way of getting Christianity into Muslim areas.

Part of our work was going into local hospitals and praying for the sick. One day in Indonesia, a friend called me and said: 'Steve, I need your help. There is someone who is very sick, and I would like you to go and visit her.'

'I'm in a pastors' meeting. I can't go,' I told him.

Despite my protests, he insisted, and I agreed to go with Detty. The sister of the sick lady took us to the hospital and told us that her sister, Winnie, had brain cancer. She wasn't a Christian.

When we got there, Winnie was lying in the bed with tubes in her nose and arms, attached to a machine that was bleeping and had flashing lights. She was very pale. Her mouth and eyes were wide open and she was staring into space. She looked like she was already dead.

'Lord, what are we going to do here?' I prayed. At that moment, my wife said, 'Good morning Winnie. My husband is a pastor, and he'd like to speak with you.'

I went over and said: 'Winnie, I want to tell you something very important. You know Winnie, there is an opportunity today for you to receive Jesus Christ as your Lord and Saviour.'

She continued to stare ahead, motionless. I told her: 'If you can hear me, squeeze my hand,' and she did. I read her scriptures and ended with Romans 10:9 'If you confess with your mouth the Lord Jesus and believe in your heart that God has raised Him from the dead, you will be saved.' I asked, 'Do you want to give your life to Jesus?' She squeezed my hand again to accept Jesus as her Lord and Saviour.

I looked around and at the bottom of her bed stood her husband and her son, who had come into the room. They were both weeping. I asked: 'Do you both need to receive Jesus as well?' They both said yes and received Jesus in that hospital room.

Winnie died two days later. I had peace in my heart because I'd taken the time to speak the word confidently and boldly and it changed her eternal destiny.

I got to know a man called Pak Andy, who broke his ankle and could barely walk. The wound was green and infected, and he badly needed an operation. A lady I knew from Singapore put her faith into action and offered to pay for surgery. Before taking him to the hospital on the day of his operation, he joined us for morning Bible study at the church's office. Anticipating the operation, he sat there smiling. When I gave him an opportunity to receive Jesus, he did and I water baptized him by full immersion in the bathtub in one of the bathrooms before taking him to the hospital, praise God! He's one of the most faithful guys you've ever seen. He managed The Diamond Project, our 'under the bridge' ministry and he also managed the medical clinic that we ran for five years to give free medicine to the underprivileged.

One day, our hospital prayer team told me that there was an English man on one of the wards called James Farrell

'Pastor, you have to go and see him,' they said.

'Well did you pray for him? You're the prayer team. Why do I have to go?'

But they were insistent, telling me that he had suffered a stroke. They want me to pray for one of my own people, I guess. I agreed to go on the way back from other visits.

James was in his mid-70's. A well-spoken businessman, he had lived in Jakarta for 15 years and married an Indonesian lady. I prayed for him in hospital and visited him in his home the next day because he couldn't afford to stay in hospital. I took two of our adopted daughters, Vonny and Indah.

While Indah sang a worship song, I said to James: 'I believe that God wants you to be saved, not just healed. He wants to give you the promise of eternal life.'

This man got gloriously saved. It was amazing.

His daughter-in-law told me that he needed to be in England under the care of the NHS because of the high cost of medical care in Indonesia. They were unable to take him to the UK because of business commitments. Later, when I shared this with Detty, I said: 'You know I feel like God's saying to me that I should take him back to England.'

When God asks you to do something, you'd better act! Otherwise, it will keep going around in your head and spirit if you don't and you might miss a wonderful opportunity.

I told James' family my proposal and they were delighted. They offered to pay for my flight ticket, which I wasn't expecting. So that Sunday, I preached in the morning and got ready for the 9,000-mile flight from Jakarta to London that night.

James was a big guy in a wheelchair and it took four of us to lift him into the car. It was nearly midnight by the time we got to the gate. I sat there, exhausted, waiting to board the plane. It had taken a lot to organise this so quickly.

'Lord, I'm tired. I just want to sleep,' I said.

'Steve, I want you to take the church to the next level spiritually, positionally, and financially,' was His response. The time and place where I least expected God to speak to me and He's talking to me about the future of our church!

We boarded the plane at the back via a special hydraulic lift and I got James settled in his seat. We were flying to Singapore, Dubai and then London.

'You okay, James?' I asked.

'Yes, I'm ok.'

I closed my eyes for what felt like 10 seconds, but when I opened my eyes, he was on the floor. He had unclipped his seatbelt and slid out of his seat, with his feet sticking through the curtains into first class! 'Oh, my goodness,' I declared and called for the flight attendants.

We got him back in his seat and eventually got to Singapore. As the plane had to be emptied for security, I asked if we could stay on because it was such a big job getting him on and off. They eventually agreed.

James got a bit anxious on the way to Dubai, so I thought I'd better give him the sleeping tablets the doctor had prescribed. But suddenly, he started singing very loudly: 'I have decided to follow Jesus...' People were looking at him, so it was definitely time for the tablets! I dropped a couple in his drink, gave it to him and waited. An hour later his chin touched his chest and I thought *Lord, he's not dead, is he?*

I took the opportunity to go for a cup of tea and a snack. I had only been gone a few minutes, but on the way back to our seats, all I could see was clouds of what looked like feathers flying up in the air. As I got nearer, I realised that James was naked in his seat! He'd taken everything off, including his adult diaper, which he had to wear after the stroke. He was plucking the foam out of the diaper and it was coming up in the air like clouds.

'James, what are you doing?' I said. *Lord what are you doing*, I thought.

On leaving Jakarta, I'd been given a changing bag for him containing diapers, talcum powder etc, for changing James en route (I had done personal care when working for the Brothers of Charity after my redundancy from UKAEA). So, when we landed in Dubai airport, I found a medical centre and asked for help in changing him. We'd been travelling for eight hours at this point.

'Sorry sir, we are emergency medical only. We don't do stuff like that.'

'But it is an emergency and he's started to smell,' I said.

They refused again and said: 'You must go to the disabled toilet and you can deal with it there yourself!' So, I grabbed a couple of attendants, got him into the toilet and lifted him out of the chair. He held himself upright on the rails in the corner and I changed him quickly and put him back in his wheelchair. It was like a Grand Prix pit stop in record time!

I text my wife and told her everything that had happened. Being German and very hygienic, I knew what her next comment would be.

'I hope you washed your hands.'

Eventually we landed in England, to be met by James' sister at the airport. She was a Spirit-filled Christian, who was over the moon that I'd brought her brother home. As neither of us knew what should happen next, I called the emergency services, who sent a paramedic on a bicycle. Soon an ambulance arrived and took him to hospital.

I had five days left in England before the return flight, so she lent me her car, gave me some money and said: 'Go and visit your family up North.' Amazing how God gives us opportunities when we are obedient to Him.

A year later Detty and I had the opportunity to return to England and we decided to visit James, who was in a Christian care home. As we were led through the home into the conservatory where he was sat, we walked straight past him because we didn't recognise him. We couldn't believe it when this slim man got up, walked towards us to give me a big hug. We were all in tears.

'Steve, you saved my life, physically and spiritually,' he said.

We went for a walk and sat on a bench in the gardens of the care home. James started sharing with Detty about the end times and about the book of Daniel. I interrupted them and said: 'James, this is just amazing. 'You had a stroke in Indonesia and got saved. I took you back to England. You've recovered. You're healed and now you're talking about the end times. I can see that you've grown up spiritually and things have happened in your life. But there's one more thing that God has for you.'

'What's that?

'He wants to fill you with His power. He wants you baptized in the Holy Spirit.'

I didn't need to say anything after that. He raised his hands and said in a loud voice: 'Lord, fill me with Your power.' And this elderly man was suddenly baptised with the power of the Holy Spirit. It was like a gushing waterfall came out of his mouth and he started speaking in other tongues. Nurses were walking past with people in wheelchairs and watching what was going on. He announced our arrival to the whole conservatory and started preaching the gospel to the residents.

He lived another three years after that, before going home to be with the Lord.

7. THE NEXT LEVEL

On returning to Indonesia after the trip with James, it was time to share what God had spoken to me about at the airport. Amazing that if I hadn't been obedient to the Holy Spirit to take James back to England in the first place, I doubt that God would have spoken to me. God always wants you to be obedient in doing what He has told you, before he will give you the next step.

Our five-year contract at Heartline Radio was coming to an end and God was sharing with us to buy land for a new building. We found suitable land about five miles away, that was in an up and coming development area. We thought it was a good investment. The land has now gone up in value about six times.

We gave everyone we knew- church members, Bible school students, those in The Diamond Project, friends, family and business connections- the opportunity to buy into this new facility and pay for bricks and cement. We had some very generous givers, but one incident that stood out was when we needed to buy 750 square metres of ceramic tiles for the floor. I said to the congregation one Sunday morning: 'How many square metres do you want to buy?' They wrote their chosen amount on pledge cards and put the cards into the offering basket. But at the end of the service, Pak Andy, who ran The Diamond Project, came to speak to me.

The people in this project live in terrible conditions under one of the main highway bridges. They live amongst rats and stray dogs, with cars zooming overhead. They have no electric, no water and no food. Some are prostitutes, but a lot of them earn just enough money for rice for that day by collecting and selling waste plastic.

We were originally invited to help these people through Youth with a Mission (YWAM). We adopted them and chose the name Diamond Project because we believe that these people are precious gems, even though they look a bit dirty and ragged. God sees the potential in each of them.

Pak Andy was concerned that the group couldn't contribute.

'Pastor Steve, you know we haven't got any money,' he said.

'It would be difficult for us individually to buy even one square metre of tiles, but we can do that as a group.'

These people had to work very hard recycling plastic cups or collecting rubbish off the streets to get this money, but they achieved it! I had tears rolling down my face. I believe that their offering was the biggest offering that was given for that facility. As with the widow in the Bible who gave all she had (Luke 21: 1-4), it's not about the amount. It's about the heart condition.

The build took 14 months and resulted in a 475-square-metre building on four storeys. It had a sanctuary that holds 500 people, a children's area, Bible school and a Connections café.

We decided on the name 'Acorn Centre' because if we had called it a church, we would have left ourselves open to be targeted in a Muslim country. There has been a lot of persecution of Christians. More than 700 churches have been burnt down and a lot of Christians killed. During Christmas 2000, four churches were blown up.

Evangelism isn't illegal, but Indonesian Christians fear that if they are reported for proselytizing (converting people from Islam to Christianity), they would get arrested. I was warned about it when I first arrived in Jakarta and was very evangelistic, but instead of making me cautious, it made me even more focused on preaching the gospel. There is a harvest beyond measure in Indonesia with many opportunities to reach the lost.

The other parts of our ministries were the Word of Faith Bible school and Seeds of Faith humanitarian project.

Before we launched our Bible school, we ran a travelling Bible school to encourage pastors to catch the vision of RBTC Indonesia.

Then the Lord told us to focus on our vision instead of theirs, so we set up our own English-speaking Bible school in Jakarta. As we were running an international church, we had some of our congregation attending the Bible school. There are a large amount of English-speaking business people in Jakarta, particularly from Australia, which is only a few hours away.

The vision of Word of Faith Bible School is to teach, train, equip and send out God's people to impact the world, starting with Indonesia. We travelled to various islands in Indonesia with teams from Singapore and America. We also taught pastors and laymen.

Under Seeds of Faith, we responded to any humanitarian and disaster relief needs that occurred. In December 2004, Indonesia was hit by the Indian Ocean Earthquake, which came to be known as the Boxing Day Tsunami. Banda Aceh was the closest major city to be affected and reported the largest loss of life - 186,000 people. But God can work in all situations and missionaries were able to go in and preach the gospel in an area that was previously shut off, being the largest Muslim country in the world.

Detty was scheduled to teach children English in Banda Aceh two weeks after the tsunami hit. She stepped out in faith to go and support them and when she arrived, she found that the children were in shock- traumatised from losing their parents and other loved ones. Through Detty showing them the love of God, they were able to experience joy and excitement in the midst of a horrible situation.

Detty speaks with a strong German accent, so I laugh when I imagine the children learning to speak English with a German accent!

In Jakarta, there was a flood in 2009, when 13 rivers overflowed and came together, forming a huge lake over parts of the city. People's homes were flooded, but thank God that where we were, there wasn't a problem.

I mobilised my church congregation and we put our love, time and finances into action. I called Noel Trinder, who headed up Hypermart, a local superstore, to ask if we could release our emergency fund to buy food for flood victims.

'Absolutely, go for it, Steve,' he said.

After ending the phone conversation, he quickly called back and said: 'Don't release the church funds. Hypermart will sponsor it all.'

They sponsored 500 emergency supply boxes that we quickly assembled, but we had no transport. I spotted a nearby truck. The driver had his feet out of the window and a newspaper on his head. This was our chance.

'Good morning,' I said. 'We need your van.'

'Cannot,' he said.

'It's for your people, who have been flooded out– we need to reach them,' I told him. He relented and within a few minutes, we filled it up and headed out.

Since there was about a foot of water on the main highway, people warned us not to go anywhere. But we went anyway. Along the way, we saw clothes still on washing lines, wet from the rain that came so quickly that people didn't have time to bring in their washing. They needed to escape the rising waters.

We found them and handed out parcels. One of them, a Muslim, was shocked at us giving parcels for free and said: 'Who are you people and why are you bringing us food?'

We told him why and this man accepted Jesus that day. We gave him one of our Living Faith caps with the Acorn logo and name and he became a living advertisement for us. We prayed that people would ask him about the cap so he could give his personal testimony.

Acorn Ministries also helped to educate children in Indonesia, including sponsoring schools. One afternoon, a pastor I knew brought an elderly man to my office, with tears rolling down his face. He ran a local school and had received an eviction notice.

'They're going to throw us out of the building! What am I going to do with 120 children?'

There was a building he wanted to rent and we took him in the car to have a look.

'I don't have any money, but by faith, we will help you,' I promised.

'We will rent it for five years and pay for all the refurbishing.'

When I got back to the church, I thought to myself *Lord, what did I just say?* Sometimes I had moments when the reality of what I'd said by faith suddenly hit me! But pretty soon money started coming in and we were able to renovate the building to become the new school.

We also purchased two community centre buildings to house an afterschool program for children and provide a place for community activities, such as patchwork and quilt making.

Over the years we've seen God provide the finances in amazing ways- the Favour of God in action again. However, it had to start with us, with our faith in God that he would provide for all our needs. We had a revelation of giving through God's word, which says, *'Give and it shall come back to you, pressed down, shaken together and running over.'* (Luke 6:38) Detty and I started sowing into different ministries and lives. As a result of our giving, a lot of money came into our ministry to meet all our needs. God saw our hearts in releasing our money into His kingdom business and He released it back into our lives and ministry.

When you give to the poor, you lend to the Lord. But when you give to the Lord, he doesn't pay back penny for penny, or at the current interest rate, which is pretty poor! He pays back hundredfold. And we were content, knowing that God had it all covered by the FOG.

It is important to let people know the ministry and personal needs, but not your wants. Many years previously, we needed £23,000 to build an orphanage for 20 children in India under Rays of Peace ministry. I shared the need in a newsletter that I emailed to supporters all over the world. What I didn't know was that God had already started talking to someone about it several months previously. The next morning, when I checked my email, some friends from Singapore had responded:

'Dear Steve and Detty. You will be amazed at how God works. A few months ago, the Lord impressed on my wife's heart that you will face a big financial need soon in your ministry and we will have to give £23,000 ($35,000) for an upcoming project. I believe that this is the project that we're looking at right now. I really feel like crying out how the Lord works and both my wife and I feel such joy at giving this sum of money away, with no struggle at all. You have my word that you will receive it as soon as possible. Let not the finances be a hindrance to your timeline in building that orphanage.'

This couple were not millionaires, just ordinary people responding in faith to God's voice, revealed to them by the Holy Spirit.

I found out later that an elderly relative had passed away years before and left them that money. They they kept in the bank and didn't know what to do with it, until that email came through.

Years ago, I was in Houston, Texas on a job assignment, when a friend of mine asked me to go to a Baptist adult Sunday school with him, before the main service. He wanted me to share about the orphanage I had been involved with in Romania and what was needed to complete it. Ten minutes later a lady approached me and said: 'My husband and I are both in business. We love to get involved with orphanages, but we're too busy to go over and help.' Then she wrote us a cheque for £400 ($521).

You see, I gave that lady an opportunity to get involved. All you need to do is tell others what God is doing in the world. Then they have an opportunity to participate and partner with you.

God still wants to stretch our faith though. One day, while preaching about money at my church during the offering, God spoke to me and said: 'Steve, get rid of the offering bucket. Don't have people come out of their seats and walk to the front or pass the offering round.' It was quite hard for me to share this in front of the congregation, but I told them: 'If you want to give, place your offering on the back table at the end of the service when we're having coffee. From now on, I'm not talking about money in this church.'

There were some shocked looks in the room that day, including my wife! She later told me she had thought *Oh my, Lord, how will we survive without tithes and offerings?*

But the biggest shock was that the offerings that day were 10 times the usual amount! The following Sunday again they were again bigger than they used to be.

Before Detty and I started the church, we were in a service listening to a well-known preacher, who runs a large church in Singapore. Afterwards, he approached us and asked: 'What are you doing here, guys? You're out in the middle of nowhere. I didn't see any other foreigners.' I explained that we were teachers at Rhema Bible Training Centre.

'I highly regard brother Hagin (RBTC founder) and I would like to give some money to your ministry,' he said.

He gave a one-off gift of £5400 ($7043) and £2000 ($2608) a month for six months. Wow! We weren't looking for this, but God knew that we needed those finances to start our church.

God is faithful. Jehovah Jireh has been and continues to be our provider. We don't have to worry about money. I remember hearing our Bible college dean, Gary Crowl say: 'If it's God's plan, then He pays and is responsible to fund His plan. If it's our plan, then we pay- we're responsible to fund our plan.' So, make sure that you're in God's plan and then you don't have to worry one single bit about where the money is coming from.

But as well as providing money and goods through faithful supporters, God has prompted them many times in prayer, which is essential for our success. People sent us emails telling us that they pray for us every day. Sometimes, I could almost tangibly feel their prayers. Those prayers help usher in the money, as well as other essentials necessary for ministry.

I remember one occasion when I felt those prayers particularly powerfully. On my first big crusade in India, I was waiting to preach before thousands of people on a big football field. It was the largest platform I'd ever been on, with a big video screen at each side and bright lights. When the praise and worship finished, I knew it was my turn to get up. The microphone seemed so far away, but as I got out of my seat, I prayed: 'Lord, there are thousands of people in front of me, but I feel so lonely.'

As I walked to the microphone, I heard the Lord say to me: 'There are many people behind you, praying for you and supporting you practically and financially. They are the behind-the-scenes missionaries. They're part of this team and this work. You are the one who has been chosen to speak, but you are not on your own.'

By the time I got to the front of the stage, I felt such a strong anointing and that night, thousands of people gave their lives to Jesus and thousands got healed. Hallelujah!

8. WE ARE FAMILY

In 2004, we started adopting girls, which became a big part of our personal ministry. The first was Reisa, a Chinese Indonesian, who came from Padang on the Sumatra island. She was 17 and her father was the pastor of a small church. She played piano and guitar and had a scholarship to study music and her parents prayed for a place for her to stay while studying, which God answered.

When she walked in our house, she said: 'I don't know what to call you. Can I call you mum and dad?' We agreed and all the other girls followed suit after that.

Reisa led worship in our church for 6 years, married a handsome Indonesian guy, Stephen, had a child and is now a music teacher at the same university she graduated from.

Ruthie came to us next, from a Muslim family in a forest village. Her Christian auntie told her about Jesus and she became a Christian. But her parents weren't happy and it caused some problems. We needed a maid and ended up employing her. She was a scrawny little thing who looked about 10 years old. She always wanted to sit in a corner on her own, but we said: 'No, you're part of our family, come and sit at the table with us.' I had to be strong with the girls in a compassionate way to encourage them to change.

One day, I said to her: 'Ruthie what is your dream?' She said she wanted to finish her education, which she couldn't do because of a lack of money. We decided to help her fulfil her dream. She stopped being our maid and we paid for her education for three years. She also learned to speak perfect English with us.

She then went onto university, graduating in hotel management. She worked in a Bali hotel for nine months, before going into teaching at an international school. She later married Ben, a church worship leader and they had two daughters. They have now opened a day care centre for babies, sponsored by Acorn.

Grace was next, who came to us six months pregnant. She had a daughter, who she called Charisma on Detty's advice- Charisma means the extension of grace. Grace became a teacher but is now the administrator of Acorn Indonesia. She is on the board of trustees, a church secretary and is going to become a pastor in the future, alongside her husband, Sadar, who is Charisma's dad. They married about six years after Charisma was born and they now have two more daughters.

We also adopted Grace's sister, Indah, who was living on the streets. She became a praise and worship leader and was a student at our Bible school for a while, but she's now doing her own thing. She's married with three children.

Jenny, our next addition, came to us aged 14 when her parents broke up. We paid for her schooling and she's now got a scholarship with a Baptist church, studies accountancy at college and works in an accountancy firm.

Our last adoption was Vonny, a Chinese Indonesian. She came to us at nine years old after the death of her father, who was a drug addict and alcoholic. Her mum had left when she was a baby.

Detty attended her father's funeral through friends and spotted this straggly little girl with a crooked haircut that looked like it had been cut with a knife and fork. She was with her Chinese grandad, who looked frail and sick. Detty approached him and asked if she could take care of Vonny. After he checked with his family, they agreed.

We went to collect her the next day from the Chines quarter in Jakarta. It was a very poor area, with open sewers and dogs roaming everywhere. Her grandad handed us a small black bag containing her belongings. All she had was two pairs of briefs and a school book.

We had no money to educate her but when we took her to church on Sunday, Rose Trinder approached us and asked who she was. She offered to support her for two years at school.

She couldn't speak a word of English at first, but now she's about to graduate in cinematography at Oral Roberts University in Oklahoma. We knew it from our time at Bible college and knew it was a Christian university. Noel Trinder, Rose's husband, continued to support her through university.

So, there I was, living in a house with nine females, including the dog! I threatened to take them all to the doctors once to get some kind of tablet that made them all have their monthly periods on the same day! It was a constant up and down of emotions, as one finished and another one started. Pain, headaches, tears and then the dog every six months coming into heat. And puppies arrived as well!

But really it was beautiful. We had Bible study every morning and evening and they all love God with all their hearts. They all took care of me, being the only guy in the house and it was lovely going out to shops and restaurants with all of our daughters. They all got on so well, because they recognised that they were all from the same situation and were like-minded. it must It must have felt like they were living in Buckingham Palace compared to where they came from.

Detty really loved and cared for them. Many times, I'd go to bed at night and she'd be there with six of them on the bed, chatting, laughing, telling stories and teaching them life skills. And I could never get on the stove, even though I'm a good cook and I enjoy it.

Every time Detty was cooking, there were seven of them behind her, all learning from her.

It cost a lot of money over the years and I've no idea where that came from. God just provided amazingly by the FOG. And I now have nine grandchildren as well!

We had our hands full caring for our girls, but one day our friend, John Harwin called and asked if we could take in two street boys, Joshua and David, who had nowhere to go. Detty said: 'I don't know about boys. I know girls, but I don't get a good feeling about starting over with boys again.'

But in the end, we agreed and they arrived on the back of a motorbike looking dirty and ragged. We cleaned them up, cut toenails, fingernails, hair, de-liced them, threw their clothes away, bought them new clothes and got them into school, which was difficult because nobody wanted them. It was a wonderful opportunity to love on people. But they were used to sleeping when they wanted, eating when they wanted and looking for money when they wanted. They couldn't cope with routine and after three months they ran away from school and our house.

A couple of weeks later they were on our doorstep, saying: 'Hi mum and dad.' They were dirty and ragged once again and we had to go through the whole process of cleaning them up.

This happened several times and one time I decided to go out and look for them one night. I spotted them with a friend and decided to take him home too because we had a spare bed in their room!

We kept trying, but it was causing a lot of unrest with our girls, even though they grew to love them and wanted to help. The next time they left they stole mobile phones, money and sold their own clothes and the bikes we gave them to buy food.

Finally, after struggling for 12 months, we asked a friend, Mike Hilliard, to take them in. He ran an orphanage, Mama Sayang, for 130 children and agreed, but he said if they ran away again, they couldn't come back.

Mike was a tough Glaswegian, ex-army who was very strict with the children and got some brilliant results. However, the boys only lasted a couple of weeks before running away and turning up at our house 24 hours later, having travelled the 75 miles with no money. They knocked on the door and said: 'Hello mum, hello dad.'

I stuck to my guns about not allowing them back in. It was one of the toughest decisions I've ever had to make, but they understood. One of them changed his surname to Laidlow as if he was a son of ours. They carried on attending church and later one of them got a job as a builder's assistant in a local school. We gave them everything, but it wasn't what they wanted. They preferred freedom and being with their friends. But I believe in the bigger picture, it did them good.

In 2007 Acorn Indonesia set up a mother and child home for pregnant young mums. These unmarried girls were referred to us by pastors, police and friends and we supported them to bring up their children, rather than have an abortion.

We had a strong Christian manager but Detty, who had a real heart for this project, took the lead on supporting these girls. She'd become pregnant herself at 15 and understood what it was like to be in that situation.

We had 11 babies over the five years that the home was running and they stayed with us for up to 18 months. The mums learned basic skills, such as baking bread in our industrial oven or making doormats. We encouraged them to start their own business or get a job. They also had to attend Word of Faith bible school, so we often had several prams in our classes, even though they weren't Christians.

We saw a number of successes. One lady went on to university. Another, Ira, who ran away at one point, is paying back as a volunteer in her home town in Manado. She became a Word of Faith student and assisted the school as an administrator.

But there were many heartaches as well. One of them was when we legally adopted a 10-day-old baby, who we named Faith. A girl in one of the Muslim communities had got pregnant and they cursed the child, hoping it would die. The mother abandoned her and she came to us. Detty commented that it was the ugliest baby she had ever seen, with infected eyes that were glued together, skin full of mosquito bites, painted on eyebrows and pierced ears with bits of string through them, which was part of the black magic cursing process.

We cleaned her up and she was soon feeding properly. However, she developed a chest infection and we nursed her, sitting up all night with her for several days. I had to go to work at 6am one day and two hours later, I received a call to say that she had died. I had to do the funeral the same afternoon.

Detty was devastated and ready to come home. Things like this don't always make sense, particularly when I'd used every ounce of faith to bring that baby back to life. As Christians we know that Jesus is the Healer, but outside of that is a lot that we don't fully understand. But we will one day.

I used to fall into bed every night exhausted, but ministry is spelt W-O-R-K. And it's very hard work. But I enjoyed every minute of it. I would do it all again. It was very rewarding, seeing people's lives turned around.

By 2008, we'd outgrown our three-bedroom rented accommodation and needed a new, larger home. For some time, I'd been driving past a run-down house in a field to get to our office and one day, God said: 'Steve, buy that house for an orphanage.' I went home and told Detty, who reminded me that we had no money and the ministry couldn't buy it.

Six month later, while driving past the house, I heard God say again: 'Steve, buy that house.' I told Detty and we decided to go and look at it. We set off down this bumpy road and when we got to the front door, we saw that half of it was rotten. I kicked the door, being a pretty rough guy and it flew open. A herd of goats ran out, followed by all their kids! I put my head inside and was hit by the smell of goat poo.

'Steve, come on, let's get out of here!' Detty wasn't impressed.

'Detty, you've got to have vision,' I told her. 'You've got to be able to see its potential.'

We tiptoed in through the goat poo and saw that the wooden window frames had been eaten by termites and there were plants growing through the walls and out of the roof.

I did some research and found out that it was owned by Chinese Indonesians. In 1998, there was a riot between the Chinese Indonesians and the indigenous Indonesians, who killed a lot of the Chinese Indonesians. Many ran for their lives, leaving property and possessions, including this house. It had never been finished and had been standing empty for 10 years.

We got in touch with the owners and made them an offer for the house, which they accepted. By faith, we arranged to sign the agreement without having the full amount of money to do it, but on the way to the lawyer's office, we had a text from a friend of ours in Singapore. He didn't even know that we were thinking of buying a house, but he asked for our bank account details to send us a love offering. It turned out to be the exact amount we needed for the deposit!

We got an architect to design it and she came up with a fantastic plan. It took about a year and every time we got a bill the money was there to pay it. I can't remember how it happened, but when it's God's will, it's His bill!

We ended up with a beautiful nine-bedroomed home, which we named The White House. It became the family home for nine of us, plus our pet beagle, Cookie and place of ministry. It was another example of the Favour of God.

One thing we didn't realise was the significance of the plot number, which was A5/35. A friend, who came to stay with us, spotted it. In biblical numbers, A is Alpha, 5 stands for God's grace or favour and 7 stands for righteousness. 7x5 is 35!

And God blessed us even more. Detty had a dream locked away inside her heart of a house with a swimming pool. We'd had a quote from the architect, and we couldn't really afford it.

A few weeks later, a little guy came to the house and knocked on the door. I looked out and couldn't see anybody- he must have been about 4 feet tall! He said he had heard that we wanted a swimming pool and he ran a company called Jonathan Pools. We invited him in and he drew up a plan, priced it up and gave us a quote that was less than half of what the architect had quoted. I looked at Detty.

'I guess you can have your dream,' I said.

The first people to go in the pool were 25 of our church members, who were water baptised, including Jonathan, who gave testimony about how he'd managed to do it at such a cheap price.

We'd never owned a house like that in England and here we were on the mission field, where people think that missionaries don't have very much and have to remain poor and needy. That's the Favour of God at work!

From left to right: Grace, Reisa, Detty, Steve, Vonny (centre), Grace (front), Indah

Back (from left to right): Stephen, Reisa, Vonny, Jenny, Grace, Sadar, Ruthie, Ben.
Front: Charisma, Steve, Detty, Rachelle

9. GOD'S BIG IN JAPAN!

We had been in Indonesia as faith missionaries for 10 years when God told us to move to Japan. We had a nice life in a lovely, nine-bedroom house with a swimming pool, a maid, gardener, driver and our seven adopted girls. We were ministering to unmarried mothers and babies. Acorn Ministries was going really well, and God was healing and saving many people. We were happy and settled.

We said to God: 'What are you doing, Lord? Why are we on the move again?' We'd said goodbye so many times in lots of different situations. It was yet another goodbye.

We couldn't speak Japanese and knew very little of the culture- only that it was at least five times more expensive than Indonesia. But we decided to go because we knew there was a great harvest field and we wanted to follow God's plan for our lives.

I'd been in Japan two years previously when the Fukushima earthquake and nuclear disaster happened. We had Japanese friends, Isamu and Natalie, who we'd met at Bible college. We located them and found out that they were safe, and I travelled over with a staff member to take emergency provisions.

We arrived in Tokyo to an empty arrivals lounge and a full departure lounge. I contacted Isamu, who was amazed that we had suddenly arrived when everyone else was leaving. He agreed to come and translate for us and we took the provisions to the affected areas.

It was horrific. I've never seen so much devastation in my life; collapsed buildings; cars on top of buildings or trees; cars compacted to matchboxes. The Tsunami wave had destroyed everything in its path. Everywhere was the smell of raw sewage, seawater and corpses. It was cold, desolate and deathly quiet– you could feel the silence and the death.

We stayed for about a week ministering to people and many got saved during that time out of their fear.

Six months later, we returned and teamed up with Samaritan's Purse, Franklin Graham's humanitarian project. We slept in tents overnight on makeshift beds, but at one point we decided to find a hotel.

We found one and asked the receptionist for a room for six people. I took the opportunity to ask her what it had been like for her in the disaster. What stuck in her mind more than anything was that her husband was screaming because he was so fearful about dying. Before I knew it, I was preaching the gospel and she gave her life to Jesus. Her husband, who was a Buddhist, came out and he got saved, then the daughter came out and she got saved. This was all in the reception area before we'd even got a room.

We got a good rate for it though!

On this visit, we travelled to Kobe to see Isamu and Natalie, who told us about their vision to pioneer a church. After returning to Indonesia, the church agreed to send me on sabbatical for two months. This was when God told me to go Japan and help them bring about their vision.

We left Indonesia on August 29th, 2013, leaving our ministry in the hands of our amazing team. Living Faith International Church is now run very successfully by pastor Sam Sisson and his wife, Nelsie.

He was a student at School of the Harvest in the Philippines, where I regularly taught at the Bible school and preached in churches.

We hadn't done any research before moving to Japan, in the same way that we didn't research Indonesia. God had told us to go and that was good enough for us. So, we said our goodbyes, left everything and set off with our two bags and a backpack in the same way we'd left the UK 10 years previously.

Once we arrived in Kobe, South Japan, we moved into a 53-square-metre apartment. It was very modern and had remote controls for everything, including the toilet! But the instructions were all in

Japanese. We had no idea what buttons to press, even to change the TV channel.

Steve and Detty settle in Kobe

Kobe, we discovered, translates as 'God's door.' We were by the ocean with mountains behind us. It has a cool, tropical climate, the sky is very often blue and there is little rain or snow. They also have amazing gardens in Japan and God knew that Detty and I loved flowers. I believe it was our reward for being in Indonesia for 10 years, where there are only two seasons- hot and very hot!

We were the only foreigners living in our area, so we had no idea what we were buying when we went to the shops. We tried to learn Japanese for six months, but it's such a hard language. There were about 3,000 main characters and 5,000 minor characters that looked nothing like our letters, so we couldn't even work them out. I hated it. I used to make excuses to go to the toilet just to get out of lessons! In the end, we gave it up. We couldn't see a purpose. We were there to assist, rather than run our own ministry.

Over the next 10 months, we helped Isamu and Natalie set up their new church. I was the Associate Pastor and helped with preaching, teaching and admin and Detty set up the children's church and trained workers.

Detty also started a part-time job teaching and training teachers at Ashyia International School and had many opportunities to minister to parents.

Japan's main religions are Taoism and Buddhism. There are many temples, but the Japanese don't worship there regularly. They are mainly used for marriages or when they want a house dedicated, which they pay the temple priest to do.

The Japanese people have a strong culture of family and there's a fear of letting go of their Buddhist and Taoism culture and following Jesus. They fear that their family will see it as not honouring their parents and they will be isolated from them and alone, maybe even cut out of the will.

Therefore, less than 1% of people are Christians and for spirit-filled, born-again believers, it's probably down to 0.5%. Isamu and Natalie felt completely isolated when they were called to Japan. I understood why God had given us the vision to help them.

The Japanese are very well-mannered and pleasant, always smiling and bowing. But they don't show emotion. They have fantastic public transport, but the people never talk on them or look at each other- apart from the funny looks I got when I accidentally got on a 'women only' train carriage!

Even the books they read in public have plain covers, so that nobody knows what they are reading. They don't want to risk appearing ignorant about any subject. The culture is very intense and focused on achievement and being pushed to the limit, but they don't want to let the mask down. There is so much suicide in Japan because people don't talk about their issues. They are smiling on the outside, but damaged on the inside.

There was one time when I did see emotion expressed. I was invited to preach at City Vision church in Yokohama, near Tokyo. I'd met Pastor Tetsuyuki Masuda and his son, Yorinori, several years previously at a seminar in Singapore. Pastor Masuda had asked if we would take care of his son when he visited Indonesia, which we did. When they heard we'd moved to Japan, they invited us to Yokohama.

It took two and a half hours on the bullet train, which is the fastest in the world. When I got there, I preached to about 50 young people about how excited supporters got in England about football and invited them to get excited about God, which they did! Four got saved and 10 re-dedicated their lives to Jesus. One boy, I remember, was 14 years old and he came to the altar sobbing and crying.

I preached again the next morning and encouraged people to come forward for prayer. The whole church came forward and I laid hands on them in the name of Jesus, not knowing what they were asking God for. There was suddenly a commotion and there were people all over the floor, all out in the Spirit. It was just amazing.

And God had planned this a few years earlier when he introduced me to Pastor Masuda. It's amazing how He brings everything together.

Another example of God's planning is that we had 50,000 'God loves you' stickers printed in Indonesia. I took a box to Japan and stuck them everywhere. What I didn't realise when we'd had them printed, is that the design, with a white background and red circle, is the flag of Japan. The design was from Arthur Blessit, who has carried a cross around the world since 1969 and put these stickers on people. I asked his permission to have the same design and he agreed, as long as we agreed to send him an Indonesian one to put on his map.

On my own map in the office, I marked out places to prayer walk, delivering leaflets and praying for each location. I also made a point of travelling further to the post office to pay bills, rather than the local shop, because I was forming a relationship with the shop assistants there, with my limited Japanese and their limited English. I invited them to our Christmas event. Nobody came, but it's my responsibility to reach out, however people choose to respond.

I also got to know the local fishermen- there's water everywhere in Japan. Once we were at a harbour with Isamu and Natalie and we started chatting to three fishermen, asking if they had caught anything. Then I suddenly felt the need to say: 'Do you know God loves you and Jesus died for you?' As my words were translated for them, one of them manifested a demon, jumping up and down (even though he had a bad leg) and ran away screaming. I never saw him again. But at least he heard about Jesus.

We kept in touch with people in Indonesia and one day, an Indonesian couple contacted me. They were coming to Japan so that the husband, who had kidney cancer, could get treated. I visited them when they arrived and prayed for the husband before the operation. I then felt led to invite them to Ikea to have a meal and a look round, to take their minds off everything.

Whilst we were eating, I started fearlessly preaching the gospel and I asked the wife, who was a churchgoer, when she had given her life to Jesus. She said she didn't think she ever had, even though she attended church and Bible studies. I led them both to the Lord at that café table. The husband collapsed on the table in tears. After that, he came to church and we prayed for him before the surgery. It was successful and he was healed.

In one of his later emails to me, he said: 'When you came to visit me in the hospital room after the operation, you were like an angel walking into my room.'

I know I'm not an angel!

God can use any means to get over the language and culture barriers. Once, when we were at a tea-tasting ceremony, there were ladies wearing beautiful kimonos with some items that looked like tissues tucked in various pockets. I started asking about them and was told they could be used for wiping your dish or writing a love letter for a friend. The Holy Spirit spoke to me and said: 'Give her a love letter.' I took one of these tissues and stuck in one of our 'God loves you' stickers, folded it and I said: 'I just want to give you a love letter.' It opened up an opportunity for us to preach the gospel and those ladies allowed us to pray for them, even though we didn't speak their language. One was in tears.

Compared to Indonesia, one of the things that took a lot of getting used to in Japan was the culture of trust. In Indonesia, there's a lot of deception, even among Christians. We eventually knew who to trust and who not to. But in Japan, it was a big culture shock having to learn to trust people again. We had a couple of people who lost their mobile phones and they turned up within a couple of days at the police station. If that was in Indonesia, they would have been sold to make money. We both had bicycles in Japan. I left my keys in my bicycle several times and each time I came back my keys and my bicycle were still there. We'd leave food items in the baskets, which would still be there when we returned.

As well as our bikes, we were blessed with a Honda, which was the smallest car I'd ever seen. Detty thought I looked like Mr Bean in it because my arms were sticking out and my knees were under my chin!

Towards the end of our time in Japan, we got a sense that it was a transition, somehow, back to England, even though we hadn't had the word from God. The culture was more British and organised than Indonesia. Rules were followed, trains were on time and they had four seasons, like England.

My dad was 88 and wasn't well and my mum, at 87, was in a care home. One day, after 18 months in Japan, the Lord said: 'Go home and take care of your parents.' It was easier to leave this time because we had nothing to hand over. And it marked the end of our time living out in the mission field and signalled another huge change in lifestyle.

10. TRAVELLING MERCIES AND THE TASTE OF CATERPILLARS!

Over the years of our travels, we've stayed in amazing places, from the richest to the poorest. We've eaten fillet steak in high-class restaurants and eaten rice with our hands, after we've laid hands on 500 people and not washed them. We've stayed in top class hotels, as well as mud huts on stilts to keep the snakes away.

Food, toilets and sleeping arrangements are a big thing in our lives, but we had to learn to be flexible and accept the cultural differences, especially where food is concerned. There are many things that are normal in those cultures that seem disgusting to us.

In China, for instance, there's nothing flying in the sky, but in the market, all the budgies, sparrows and starlings are lined up on sale for food.

I once asked my interpreter, Jim, about Chinese food.

'I've heard that you eat cats and dogs in China', I said.

'Actually, two days ago, we had cat' he replied.

'You mean me and you?'

'Yeah, that restaurant we were in the other day.'

I was convinced I'd eaten chicken. It certainly tasted like chicken!

'So, have you ever eaten dog?'

'Not my own dog!' He sounded offended.

'Only my friend's dog.'

Another time, while working on a factory floor fitting machinery, I suddenly spotted the biggest rat I'd ever seen- bigger than a cat! It disappeared underneath a metal plate.

'A big rat just went down there,' I said to one of the other workers.

'Mm, yum yum,' he said, lifting up the metal plate. Underneath there was a rat trap, containing the cat-sized rat. He took it out of the trap and dropped it in his bag, licking his lips.

'We'll have that for dinner tonight.'

I liked to challenge myself to eat certain things to prove that I'm a missionary. But I also wanted to be able to relate to the people. And you can really offend some if you refuse their food.

In the Philippines I ate a balut, which is a duck egg with the baby duck still inside. You eat all of it- bones, beak and feathers. It was very crunchy and I was spitting feathers! I managed half and gave the other half to my friend, who finished it and then threw up on the floor. Closing your eyes while you eat it often an advantage in Asia!

When I was in Thailand working with pastor Luke, his mother-in-law passed away and I was asked to do the funeral. After a procession through the forest with chanting, singing and dancing, we returned to the house for a big party and food. We looked at it. There were tree caterpillars the size of your finger. And they were still moving! Detty nudged me and said: 'I'm not eating them!'

'I'm a missionary,' I told her. 'I'm going to try them.' It had probably taken a week to gather them all and they were so happy to serve this delicatessen to us.

So, by faith, I put one of these huge, sausage-like caterpillars in my mouth and chewed it. Everything burst in my mouth. I swallowed it, smiled at Pastor Luke and said: 'Great!' If John the Baptist could eat locusts, I could eat tree caterpillars!

Sometimes food is unpleasant for different reasons. I tried Kobe beef, in Japan, which is world-famous. They massage the cows and play classical music to them to calm them and improve the quality of the beef. It's very expensive, but I thought it was horrible- very fatty tasting.

Drinks can be just as challenging. In Africa, we were told: 'You're English. I'm sure you'd love some tea.' So, they made us some and I've never in my life had tea like it! The milk and tea were boiled together, and it had white froth on top. It also tasted like there was a full 1kg bag of sugar in it.

However, in Japan, the tea is very different- thick, like oil and very bitter. The Japanese have a lot of tradition around drinking tea. They put it in a bowl and you have to hold your hands in a special way around it and slurp it. The more noise you make the more it demonstrates that you like it.

One thing I refused to drink pretty early on was alcohol, which I haven't drunk since 1995. At the time I was on commission in Thailand and went to a restaurant one evening. I was reading a book on the end times, while drinking a glass of beer. I was a married man and a new Christian, but I remember thinking how pretty the waitress was. When I finished that beer, I asked for another one and as I drunk it, she started looking even prettier. I started thinking about what might happen and then suddenly I looked at my beer and realised that this was the reason my mind was changing.

I'd also witnessed a lot of drink driving and domestic incidents and crime connected to alcohol when I was in the special constabulary and I decided that there was no way I was going to allow alcohol to alter my mind. I didn't even finish it and I haven't touched a drop since. I don't miss it because I know the effects of it- so many people become addicted because they like the effect. And just think of all the money I've saved!

Toilet facilities can be just as varied and challenging. The ones in Japan are amazing. They are all singing all dancing, with heated seats in winter and all kinds of water jets operated from a control panel. There's even a button for people with upset stomachs. It plays music to disguise toilet noises! But in India, you ask where the bathroom is and they give you a spade and say: 'It's the third bush on the left.'

Different cultural attitudes can also be a challenge. One time when I was in Thailand with Ruel Morgan, we were in a bamboo hut. I preached to about 50 people and Pastor Luke interpreted for me. He suddenly said: 'I've got to go to the toilet.' Well, I expected him to go off to the bathroom, but he went to the other side of a small bamboo screen on the platform, where we were preaching. The noise was as loud as a woodwind orchestra! I couldn't believe it.

I looked at Ruel and said: 'I think we should sing a song.' I got him to the front and we sang: 'I have decided to follow Jesus...' Neither of us can sing so it wasn't very good, even though it was a joyful noise unto the Lord! And it took the congregation's mind off what was happening. Then suddenly Pastor Luke appeared as if nothing had happened, smiled, zipped up his trousers and we carried on!

Every time I travelled, I prayed that God would provide opportunities to share Jesus with people. I was once travelling to Thailand on business one Sunday and on the way to the airport, I started sharing Jesus with the driver. He said: 'Wow! I've never heard about anything like that before.' I asked him if he would be willing to go to our church and he said yes. I told him to go back to my house and I called Detty to let her know that he was coming back.

She took him to church while I was at the airport waiting for the flight. She told me later that during the sermon, he kept asking Detty lots of questions like: 'What is he talking about? Who is our Heavenly

Father? Why does He love me?' When there was an alter call, Detty asked him if he would like to go forward and he said: 'Not on my own. You come with me.' Some people need a little bit of a hand sometimes. So she guided him to the altar and then they went into the altar care room, where there was a support team.

After a couple of minutes somebody came out and said: 'We need an Arabic translator. This man does not understand what we are sharing from the word of God and we need to teach him before we lead him to Jesus.' Now at this point we were attending Rhema Bible Church in the middle of Broken Arrow, Tulsa, in Oklahoma. It's like the ends of the earth! It had the biggest sky I'd ever seen in my life. There was so much land.

Detty went outside the church, which was nearly empty because the service had finished and prayed for God to send someone. Suddenly, a man, with his wife and children came rushing around the back of the church. Detty said: 'Do you speak Arabic?'

'Yes'

'Wow! We need you in the altar care room.'

The husband told her that they just wanted to shake hands with Pastor Hagin, but Detty was insistent. He agreed, came to the altar care room and as a result the Arabic taxi driver gave his life to Jesus.

Meanwhile, I'd boarded the plane from Tulsa to Chicago and found myself sat next to a very pretty lady in a fur coat, with amazing hair and make-up. I asked her where she was going and she said she was attending a make-up seminar in Chicago. She asked me where I was going, so I told her and before I knew it, I was sharing my testimony about how God changed my life and the work I did with the orphanages in Africa and India. She never said a word and she never got out of her seat. On airplanes, people can't get away. This makes for the perfect divine opportunity to preach the Word! Detty and I have many experiences of people giving their lives to the Lord on the airplane.

When I mentioned the scripture John 3:16, she said: 'Do you know you're the third person in six months to tell me about God?'

'I believe God is trying to get your attention,' I said.

'Yes, I think you're right.'

I got my Bible out, read her the scripture in full and she listened with tears in her eyes. I asked her if she wanted to be saved and when she said yes, I led her to the Lord there and then. She didn't have waterproof mascara on and her make-up was running down her face! But she was so happy.

After she cleaned up her makeup, she put some money into my hand as we were getting ready to leave the plane.

'I don't charge for my services you know,' I said.

'No, it's for the orphanage in India that you told me about.'

Sometimes God has enabled journeys to take place as part of His plan. Once, when we were at Bible college in Singapore, my brother-in-law emailed me. He wasn't a believer, but he wanted me to pray for his mother, who had cancer and had only been given six months to live.

I suggested that some of our friends in that area could go and pray with her, but he said: 'No way! This is a family thing and I'm just asking you to pray.' So we prayed for laborers and God intervened. A friend of mine, John Yeo, came to me and said: 'I want to go to England to check out some equipment and I need somebody who's English to show me around. Would you come with me?' I agreed and he paid for the flight, hotel and food. Two days later he said: 'My wife wants to go so we'd like to invite Detty as well. We'll pay for Detty's flight and her hotel and food.' Free trip to England- praise the Lord!

Where he wanted me to go was about 50 miles from our home town, where my brother-in-law's mother was. We went to visit her and she gave her life to Jesus. And a couple weeks later she died.

But everywhere we go, we're representing God as his ambassadors. Once I was on a three-day mission trip in Bengkulu, on the west coast of Sumatra with my friend, Bernie Berg, from Canada. When we came back to the airport, we were told that the flight was cancelled.

'What do you mean the flight's cancelled– we've got our tickets here,' I said.

'The local Mayor's daughter is getting married and they've taken over the plane.' We were gobsmacked. But even worse, we were told that we had to be out of our hotel because they wanted to use that as well! And we couldn't get another flight for three days.

The next day we came back. And we came back strong.

'We want our flight today.'

'Sorry sir,' we were told

'Do you know that we're ambassadors?'

It totally changed then! We were taken to the VIP room and given refreshments. An official came in and asked to see our passports.

'It says here you're British and Canadian citizens,' he said. 'I thought you were ambassadors.'

'No, we're ambassadors for God.'

'Get out of here!'

We didn't get our flight and were stranded for three days. It was a good try though!

11. FINDING PURPOSE THROUGH THE PAIN

After leaving Japan and our missionary lives, we arrived back in England on January 27th, 2015. It felt strange not to be in ministry. I'd been looking after churches and preaching most Sundays for 15 years. I loved the mission field, with all its 'James Bond' kind of adventures, doing things that most Christians don't get an opportunity to do.

My dad was very sick. I'd prayed for him for 25 years to receive Jesus and preached the gospel until I was red in the face, but he didn't receive it.

I visited him in hospital and suddenly felt such an anointing of the Holy Spirit. I had taken my old Gideon bible off the shelf before visiting and I didn't know why at the time. I showed it to him.

'Dad, do you recognise this Bible?'

'No,' he said.

'Well you should do because you gave it to me in 1963 at my confirmation. And this is your handwriting isn't it?' It had something like 'with love on your communion day' written in it. I read him Psalm 23 and he was mouthing the words. I think he'd learned it from my grandfather, who was a Christian. I told him it was a promise that only some people receive. I read him several other

Scriptures and asked him if he wanted to receive Jesus as his Lord and saviour and he said yes. Two days later he died, aged 89.

I took his funeral service and told all my family how he was saved. They were gobsmacked. They had tears rolling down their cheeks.

We'd moved into mum and dad's bungalow on our return, where they had lived for the last 40 years. My sister, Janet, had lived around the corner for the same length of time. I'd done work on the house for them over the years and Detty and I started renovating it by replacing the kitchen. She helped me rip out the old kitchen– that's how fit she was before she became ill.

Later that year, my mum passed away. I had the assurance that she was in heaven because four years earlier, God gave me an opportunity to lead her to the Lord when I was visiting England. At the time, dad was going to hospital for a check-up and he asked me to take care of mum. The anointing came to me and I said: 'Mum, I'm going to tell you some information that I've never told you before.' I got my Bible out and I shared the gospel with her. Thirty minutes later there were tears and forgiveness as she gave her life to Jesus. It was very emotional for both of us.

Not long after mum's death, Detty started having a persistent cough. She went to the doctor twice and was referred for an X ray, which confirmed that there was a shadow on her lung. She then had an MRI and the results came back: she had lung cancer in one side of her lung.

That was the last thing we had expected and it was a shock. We'd never known anyone with cancer and being overseas we'd lost touch with the UK.

The consultant told us that they could remove part of the lung and there was a good survival rate in those cases. Five days later they called and asked her to come in the same day for the operation and we were praising God for the VIP treatment.

It was major surgery, but when she came round, the pain and the cough had gone. The surgeon told us that he had managed to remove all the cancer. After ten days in intensive care, she came home to rest and slowly regained her strength as I took care of her. We thought that was the end of it.

Then in February 2016 she received a letter asking her to go in for chemotherapy. We thought that the cancer had been removed, but we were told that they were taking precautions in case a few cells had been missed.

We had no idea about the effects of chemo. It was all new to us. We were just believing God for a miracle like we'd seen in so many others.

She was due four cycles. The first and second cycles zapped her, made her really ill and she spent most of the time in bed. I had to call the ambulance twice to take her to hospital and I believe it nearly killed her. She was put on a lower dose for the last two cycles.

I had no idea what stage cancer this was. They could have said that it's stage 156 and we would have said: 'Praise the Lord.' We weren't focused on numbers, didn't research cancer or read any of the booklets we were given. We were just focused on the fact that God was going to do a miracle and would use it as a witness for him.

Detty was absolutely on fire for God throughout. She was the best evangelist you'd ever hope to meet, talking to everyone, even in the hospital about Jesus, saying: 'You just watch this. There's going to be a miracle and the medical profession will be shocked.' Only once or twice did she have a dip, but she was soon back on top again quickly. She was a very strong lady with a secure faith in God.

Once the chemo was over, we had a bit of a 'hallelujah party', praising God that it was finished. But then another letter came asking Detty to have radiotherapy every day for two weeks. It was painful going to the hospital all the time, because it brought home the reality of what was happening. We don't normally see the big picture of the hundreds of people going through that hospital or the thousands passing away every day. We just get on with our lives.

Vonny came back from America just before her summer break from Oral Roberts university and we decided to go to Scotland- a place that Detty loves. We saw it as a time of recuperation and a celebration that the surgery, chemo and radiotherapy was all now over and healing could begin. What we didn't know was that it would be her last visit.

We took a coach trip and Vonny, who was in her late teens then, was bored out of her mind being amongst all those old people! We enjoyed it, but Detty didn't have the strength to walk, so we hired a wheelchair.

Travelling home on the M6 she said: 'I feel like I should give my testimony.' She was very determined, so we got her to the front of the bus and gave her the coach driver's microphone. Holding onto the rail, she pulled herself up, gave her testimony, preached the gospel and gave an alter call! There were people all around me crying and responded. It was amazing.

Detty's sister had passed away six months before and we'd flown over to Germany for the funeral. Even though she wasn't well, the anointing came on her in the service and she was preaching the gospel and giving an alter call in a Catholic church! The priest was cringing in his seat.

After returning from Scotland, we planned another trip to Kent to visit friends. She really wasn't well while we were there and she had to have a bed in the lounge, because she couldn't go upstairs. She suddenly developed pain in the top of her thigh and when we got back to Preston, she couldn't get out of the car and I had to help her in the house.

The next day I called an ambulance and even though she wanted to stay at home, I encouraged her to go hospital. As they took her out of the house in her wheelchair, she waved to one of the neighbours. That was the last time she was ever at that house.

They X-rayed her leg and asked her how she had broken it. We were both really surprised. There had been no accident or anything. She'd broken her femur and the scan showed that the cancer had gone into her bones and they had just crumbled.

We were told not to worry because they could do a hip replacement, which she had a few days later. She had the operation under local anesthetic and when she came out of theatre, she had an oxygen mask on. She became totally reliant on it.

I had a visit from the palliative care team who asked if she'd done everything in life that she'd wanted to do. But the penny still didn't drop and I was chatting away about our recent trips. Then suddenly it hit me like a bomb what they were saying.

We'd just got a Labrador puppy, called Toffee, which Detty encouraged me to buy. I was resisting because I know what a tie dogs can be, but Vonny was also encouraging me, even though she was at university in America. We decided to get one and I said to the care team that Detty hadn't yet seen the dog. They had a word with the matron who agreed we could bring it in. I was shocked and so was Vonny. But she put the dog in her backpack and brought it to hospital with my sister, who had been caring for Vonny in our absence. Everyone was staring at them because Vonny came in wearing the backpack on her front with the dog's head sticking out!

Detty was completely conscious but couldn't speak. We put the dog on the bed and this seven-week-old puppy, as lively as anything, just curled up on her leg and she stroked it for about two hours. It was almost like the dog knew what was happening.

The day before she died, our church pastor came and started reading from his Bible. Detty signalled for him to stop. She got hold of my T shirt, dragged me to the bed and wrote on my T shirt 1-2-1 with her finger. I realised what she wanted: Psalm 121. It said: 'I lift my eyes up to the hills, where does my help come from? It comes from the Lord.' Spiritually, she was still very much alive, even though her body was failing. There was no fear, no doubt or anything. She was praising the Lord and it was amazing.

The next day the consultant told me she was not going to make it. I was shocked. Within a couple of hours, on July 31st, she had passed away with me and my sister by her bedside. She was just 57 years old.

In the months after her death, I cried a lot and couldn't sleep. I cried out to God, saying: 'Lord, what happened? You could have used her as a mighty testimony for Jesus. All you had to do was heal her like we've seen you do so many times. Why all the people we'd prayed for and not Detty?' It didn't make sense, especially as neither of us had been ill in all the years we'd been on the mission field. And suddenly, this happened.

I really couldn't understand why He didn't intervene. But eventually I came to the understanding that I don't know what God's will was in that area. Maybe He's got her organising heaven because she was such a great organiser!

But the revelation I've come to is from 1 John 5:14, which says *'This is the confidence we have in approaching God, that if we ask anything according to His will, He hears us and He answers our prayers.'* It wasn't about my will and the will of all the people around the world praying for her healing, but about God's will in this situation.

In a spiritual sense, she was totally healed because she's in heaven. We tend to put everything in the physical realm, but this has really changed my perspective. It's still on the shelf and I guess one day I will find out why. We're all going to pass away from this earth at some time in our life, but we don't know where, how and when.

It was an incredibly difficult time for me. In the space of 18 months I'd lost my dad, my mum, my sister-in-law and my Auntie Ruth. And my first wife had also died from cancer a couple of months before my dad died.

Even though I didn't understand, it strengthened my faith because the Lord brought me through that time of grief and made me stronger as I relied on Him. The Bible says when we are weak, we are strong and I'm now ministering from the experience I had. I've led about 90 funerals since Detty passed away, under my new ministry, Life Tributes. It's really therapeutic for me to share my story with those who have lost loved ones and tell them that I know how they are feeling. They realise that I'm telling the truth and can relate to their suffering. I can also share how God has strengthened me through it all.

Detty's funeral, at Longton Methodist Church, was fantastic. We had people from all over the world and the church was full to bursting point. We had a live praise and worship band and there was such joy because she'd gone to heaven. I didn't want it to stop.

Non-believers who attended said they'd never attended anything like that and the pastor said why can't every church service be like that funeral service.

One of Detty's brothers asked if I would speak at his funeral because he wanted it to be just like this one.

Detty's life had blessed so many people. Without her I wouldn't have even become a Christian, gone to Bible school or gone to Indonesia. She followed me around the world and I loved her for her faith.

While Detty was going through her illness, we found out that our friend, Rose Trinder, who supported Vonny through school, was diagnosed with exactly the same strain of lung cancer as Detty. Her and Rose talked by text and phone about their experiences, as both myself and her husband, Noel did. She died nine months after Detty and I spoke at her funeral in Perth, Australia.

I was unsure whether to stay in mum and dad's house or not. My mind was like a whirlwind. But on Detty's birthday on October 19th, I took some flowers to her grave at St Andrew's Church, Longton. It was a beautiful day- sunny and calm. There wasn't a soul in the whole graveyard. I stood by the grave and said: 'Lord, should I move or should I stay?' I heard very clearly: 'Move.'

I went home, called an estate agent who came around that afternoon. That night the house was on Right Move and the next day a man wanted to visit. He had also just lost his wife and his daughters lived round the corner. He wanted what I was selling- a small bungalow with two bedrooms and open views at the back. Within 24 hours, I'd sold it!

That evening I went on Right Move again. I'd been looking for a couple of months, wondering if I should move or not. I was considering Garstang, where my son, Greg lived with his wife and three children.

I'd already looked at every house in the area within my price range. But suddenly a house came up that I'd never seen before. I arranged to visit it the same night.

The house had things in it that Detty and I had spoken about putting in my dad's house, like a visitor's toilet, bi-folding doors onto the garden and an extension. I got my son round that night to look at it with me.

'Why do you want a four-bedroomed house?' He was puzzled.

'I don't know,' I responded.

I decided to make an 'Indonesian' offer, which was ridiculously cheeky- £50,000 below the asking price. I just plucked a number out of the air really. Within an hour, they called back and accepted it! So, within two days, I'd heard from God to move, put the house on the market, sold it and bought another one! But that's the Favour of God again. It's always there for us to receive, even in the darkest of times.

I moved in six weeks later, just before Christmas. I didn't have much to move because we'd come from overseas in our usual way, with two bags and a backpack.

Acorn Indonesia had always continued, but I thought Acorn UK would end when we came home. Several volunteers needed to retire or move on and it was all on my shoulders. I was going to close it down, but when I started taking mission trips out again, I saw how valuable it was for people to step out of their comfort zone and have a taste of mission, so I decided to keep it going.

I've taken lots of teams out and sometimes people are thoroughly miserable and say they hate the food and hate the climate.

'Praise the Lord,' I tell them.

'Why do you say that? I've been crying for 10 days.'

'Now you know that you're not called to do this.'

Others say: 'I could do this every day of my life.' Again, I say: 'Praise the Lord.'

You need to have a taste of things to know if you like them.

The first time I returned to the Philippines and Jakarta, everything reminded me of Detty. That was sometimes painful, but it also brought joy to see the legacy she'd left behind and the people's lives she had touched and changed. The more I went back there, the more I saw it. Maybe it will be the same when I pass away and people will see my legacy.

12. SEE I AM DOING A NEW THING!

In January 2018 I got a revelation from God. He gave me Isiah 43.18, which says, *'Forget the former things; do not dwell on the past. See, I am doing a new thing! Now it springs up; do you not perceive it?'* God was saying: 'Steve, it's time to move on.'

It's awful when people go out of your life like that. But this was a new season. We can't change our past, but we can change our future. It really helped me and I started to come out of the tunnel and towards the light at the end.

God started speaking to me about setting up a Word of Faith Bible school in Preston, using the same teaching syllabus as before, offering 25 subjects. That was my re-instatement and it was launched on September 3rd, 2018. We started with five instructors from around the North West, teaching 15 students. We also offer teaching by correspondence for some who can't travel in as often.

Over the summer, I'd been marketing the new Bible school and a lady called Andrea Branson, who attended Kings Church in Blackpool got in touch. She'd seen a flyer and wanted to meet me to discuss it further. I met her one lunchtime and she was really keen. She messaged me a couple of days later and said she had talked to her pastor, who wanted to meet me to check me out! I said no problem and I would come to the church the following Sunday.

I'd never even heard of Kings. I walked into the church, which was then meeting at the Vue Cinema, Cleveleys and I was thinking *this is a pretty neat church with this huge screen!*

I'd seen the pastor, Ann Strickland, at the front and we met later that day, when she grilled me! She was very strict and thorough at finding out about my credentials as a Bible teacher. She gave her blessing for Andrea to attend the school, so I must have done a good job!

She said if I needed to chat further, Andrea would pass on my number, which she did. I called pastor Ann and asked to meet up, so we met for coffee and I told her that I would like to submit to her leadership and become part of Kings church.

I started attending Kings and I kept bumping into Pastor Ann at various meetings and social events. We got on very well, both being ministers and it was all just friendly and relaxed, not talking about our past, future or any kind of relationship.

One day, we were talking by text and she told me that her car had broken down. As an ex-engineer I started being a diagnostic checker and asking various things about it, but eventually she had to call the AA. She should have been going to a family funeral in Manchester.

I told her that I hoped she could get it fixed and left it at that. But the Holy Spirit said to me: 'Take her to the funeral.' And I'm thinking *you want me to take the pastor of the church to a family funeral? Really?*

I took her there and met her family. I scored some great brownie points that day, even though it wasn't my motive at all!

I found out that Monday was her day off and I asked if she fancied doing something. We went to the cinema at the Flower Bowl in Preston to watch 'The Greatest Showman' and that was the turning point in our relationship. That film is so uplifting and has a Christian ethos behind it of helping underprivileged people.

She was planning a trip to Spain to visit her sister Mary and I was going on mission for two months. She told me that she was going to the Lake District the weekend before going to Spain. It was normally a family holiday every year with about nine people, but for various reasons, they couldn't go. She decided to go alone because she'd booked a fortnight off for the first time in 10 years and needed a break. I suggested coming up for the day and having a coffee with her.

On the morning she was going to the Lakes, she was praying and worshipping in her apartment and she heard the voice of God behind her, saying: 'Today, Steve's going to ask you to marry him.' And she said: 'If he does, I'll say yes, because I love him.' She carried on worshipping, before setting off to the Lakes.

Meanwhile, I was driving to the Lakes to meet her and I heard the Lord say: 'Ask Ann to marry you today.' I said: 'What?' I even opened the window to get a bit of fresh air, I was so surprised. Oh, my goodness, I'd never anticipated doing that! I knew I would want to marry again one day and didn't want to spend the rest of my life alone, but Ann, who had been married before, was so focused on her ministry and never wanted to marry again.

We met and had coffee and she read out a poem to me, which she'd written the day before:

Dedicated to my special man that God sent
27th September 2018

When I think of you,
My body tingles too.
I dream of what could be,
Following the wanderer over sea.

As a woman I've come alive,
You've opened the lid now I'll thrive.
Please handle my heart with care,
From the past it had a great tear.

I'll entrust all I am to you,
On the day that I say: 'I do'.
I'll follow wherever you lead,
Safe and secure in your arms I'm freed.

Serving our God together,
Here there or wherever.
It's the greatest joy of man,
Coming together in our Saviour's plan.

As we've heard His voice,
And we've made our choice.
Let the adventures begin,
Whatever comes we'll take it on the chin.

I've never felt this way before,
Your love has opened up the door.
My heart is overflowing love,
May it flow to you on the wings of the dove.

Annie

After listening to her poem, I simply said: 'Ann, will you marry me?' And she said yes straight away. We were both blown out of our seats and almost jumped vertical! I had no ring or anything and it hadn't been part of the conversation up to that point. But we were both so happy. And then it all came out very quickly that God had spoken to both of us that morning.

I joined Anne on the boat trip she had planned across Lake Windermere and as we sailed, I said: 'Where are we going to get married? We don't have a church. We're still in the cinema.' I spotted a lovely venue on the side of the lake, called Storrs Hall.

'Why don't we get married there?'

'I can't believe what you are saying,' she said. 'That's my favourite place in the whole of the Lake District!'

I had no idea it was a wedding venue! I guess it was the Holy Spirit again prompting me.

After the boat ride, Ann asked where we were going.

'Storrs Hall,' I told her.

'What, right now?'

'Well we're getting married there aren't we?'

Once inside we sat down with another coffee, the wedding application form and brochure and within an hour had designed the service, guest list- everything! On the way out we handed in the application form with the date- January 3rd, 2019.

The wedding planner wasn't in, so I called her the next day to pay the deposit. She said she would need to check if the date was available. I thought she doesn't need to check. It's already available by faith! She checked and said: 'Guess what, it is available.'

'I knew it would be,' I said and paid the deposit right away.

That was on the Friday and on Monday I drove her to the airport to travel to Spain and I went off on mission the following Thursday. We were constantly in contact and planning the wedding. We were both walking on air and very happy. Not a single doubt ever came, because we both just knew it was from God. When you know the voice of God, it's so easy. What was the point of waiting?

We found out at some point that Andrea Branson had been praying with her friend, Kathy Roper, since the previous New Year's Eve, for a husband for their pastor. Andrea Branson was a big part of all that. Also, Ann's sister, Mary told us in the address at our wedding that she'd been praying for 'a drop dead gorgeous George Clooney look alike, wads in the bank, not intimidated by strong women, treats you like a princess and loves God with all his heart....well four out of five isn't bad!'

The wedding was like a dream come true and I had such an amazing sense of peace. Kings Senior Pastor Derek Smith married us, my son, Greg was my best man, Ann's brother, Mike Walsh gave her away and her daughter, Louisa was her chief bridesmaid.

We had about 80 guests, including Vonny, from university in America and Grace and Ruthie came from Jakarta.

After our honeymoon, we also had a wonderful celebration at the Imperial Hotel, Blackpool, with 240 friends and church members to share in our happiness.

Ann has said that she's never been as happy, had as much fun, laughed as much and never felt so at home as she does now.

And I now know why I bought a four-bedroomed house, because my wife has got so much stuff!

Ann and Steve Laidlow

Once again, I've experienced the Favour of God, through Him bringing me an amazing lady, beautiful inside and out.

And we are about to go on a two-month mission together! God released Ann from a fear of returning to the mission field after a previous trip had left her wheelchair-bound when she contracted M.E. I had asked her to give the keynote speech at the opening of the new Bible school in September 2018. It was on a Monday, which was her day off, but she agreed to do it, although she told me later that she was thinking *why am I saying yes when I mean no?*

After her speech, God spoke to her and told her to operate in faith not in fear and challenged her to go on mission, which she agreed to do. What she didn't know at the time is that she would be going out with the Bible teacher, who would by then be her husband!

As part of our trip we're attending the wedding of my friend, Noel Trinder, in Australia. His wife, Rose, died from the same strain of lung cancer as Detty and now he's getting married to a lovely Vietnamese lady. He was originally going to marry on the same day as myself and Ann, but it was delayed because of immigration paperwork. However, it now means that I'm going to be there to celebrate his special day, with my wife alongside me, praise God!

Looking back over the time since I became a Christian at the age of 43, I'm amazed at everything God has done in my life. There have been many challenges, heartaches and moments when I've wanted to give up, but some incredible blessings, breakthroughs and miracles. God has always been faithful to His promises as I was faithful to His calling. And it was only by getting out of the boat and walking on the water that I've experienced the amazing Favour of God. I'm excited for this new chapter in my life and pray that my story will inspire you to step out of your own comfort zone and experience the extraordinary life that is available to every believer.

PART 2. THE FAVOUR OF GOD IN YOUR LIFE

1
FOR I KNOW THE PLANS I HAVE FOR YOU

saiah 1:19 says, *'The willing and the obedient, they will eat the good of the land.'*

God has amazing plans for you. Think about it; this awesome, incredible indescribable God, who created the heavens and the earth, the fish in the sea, the birds on the air, all the animals, and all the people who live on the earth has a plan for your life! Wow!

If you put God first in your life and follow His plan, you will be amazed at how God can use you. He will bless you abundantly, beyond your wildest dreams. He will give you opportunities to go places and meet people that you never ever dreamed of. You couldn't even dream of it because the plan is so big!

I never thought that I would go to so many countries and have such amazing experiences in my time of being a Christian. But I knew God's purpose for my life and He has a purpose for you as well. In the years to come, you'll be telling stories just like I have in this book, providing you are willing and obedient to take action.

The biggest lie on the planet is that when I get what I want I will be happy. The devil will try to tell you that, particularly around money and success. Only God's plan for your life will make you truly happy.

What are your dreams? What is the visions God has given you? Pray out the plans and purposes of God for your life; pray in the Spirit; pray out mysterious things that you don't know about! I guarantee God will speak to you as He did to me. He will give you direction. He will reveal His plan and purpose to you. All you have to do is tell God that you are willing, available and will be obedient when He speaks.

In 2 Chronicles 16:9, it says, *'For the eyes of the Lord search throughout the earth, looking for people who are fully committed to Him.'* God's watching you. When He sees that you are fully committed to Him, He will start to speak to you and open doors that no man can close.

God wants to do a new thing in my life and yours. We can't change the past, but we can change the future. Just look at what the Lord has already done in your life, and then think about what He is going to do, because God is a God of new beginnings and fresh starts. If you reflect back on your life before you were saved, I'm sure you can see the development, the maturity and the growth in your life. We're changed by the death and the burial of the resurrection of Jesus Christ. We're changed forever.

Move forward with God and don't look back. God is going to thrust you into areas you never thought of going, if you walk by faith. The Holy Spirit will lead you and show you step by step of things to come.

God's not going to reveal the next part of the plan until you are faithful with what He's already called you to do, whether that's stacking chairs in church or standing at the door greeting people. In Acts 9: 6 it says, *'Now get up and go into the city, and you will be told what you must do.'* Here we see that Paul had to go first into the city before God gave him further instructions. Paul had to be obedient to God.

We often look for guidance in our own lives, but many times we ought to do something by faith before God tells us the next step. Think of a little boy. He asks his dad if there is anything he should do. His dad tells him to clean up his room. One hour later the boy asks his dad again if there is anything he should do, but he still had not cleaned his room. Do you think that the dad will give him anything else to do before he cleaned his room? No, the child has to do first what the father told him to do and then he will give him other things to do.

Paul had to go to the city first and the little boy had to clean his room first. What about you? Are there things God told you to do and you haven't done them? And yet, you are waiting for the next assignment from God. Think about the things in your life that God is dealing with right now. Bring them before God and ask for forgiveness. Once you have done what He asked you to do then trust God for the ext step.

While you're being faithful in the small things, it's also about getting to know God more and deciding to trust Him with your future. He wouldn't give us more than we could cope with.

I encourage you to read 'Run with the Vision' by Lester Sumrall. Mr. Sumrall wrote that book with the Lord's final harvest in mind. The following quote from this book captures God's view of us, the body of Christ:

A mind open to any way to reach the world with the gospel;
Ears that always listen to God's voice;
Eyes that see the need in the world and in their own backyard;
A heart that goes out to the people who don't know Jesus;
Elbows equipped with lots of elbow grease to pitch in wherever needed;
Pockets open to give generously to people in need;
Knees bent over to pray for missionaries;
Feet that go wherever God leads at home or abroad;

Children: junior partners in spreading the gospel, and
Hands that write letters, build buildings, bandage wounds, cook meals
or put in the skills to work for God's purpose.

You know the Bible says that Jesus is coming back but we don't know the hour and we don't know the day. Not even angels, not even Jesus knows. It will be like a twinkling of an eye and like a thief in the night. But my vision is to be caught in the very act of fulfilling God's plan on this earth, not laid on the sofa watching Manchester United!

I believe that God is going to ask us some important questions when we meet Jesus face to face. We will have to give an account of our lives and He will ask us what we did with the resources and finances He put into our hands. He will also ask: 'What did you do with the gifts and the talents that I gave you? Did you use them for My glory? Did you use them to build My kingdom? Or did you keep them hidden in your pocket?'

Another question I believe He's going to ask us is: 'What did you do with the name of Jesus? Did you keep it and say: 'Hallelujah! I'm going to heaven. Praise God. I'm so excited' or did you use the name of Jesus with all power and all authority? Did you go into all the world? Did you lay hands on the sick? Did you cast out demons in the powerful name of Jesus?'

Don't limit God. Don't tell God what you will or will not do or where you will or will not go. For instance, don't say that you don't want to go overseas, or to this community or that project. Focus on the plan and say: 'Father, show me, lead me, guide me by your Holy Spirit.' But don't resist it when He tells you. He knows our gifts. He knows our talents and how He can use us best. We are like the many pieces in a jigsaw puzzle. Where are you in that jigsaw puzzle? What is your part to play in the big picture?

God will use you right where you are today. You don't need to do anything else for God for Him to use you right now. You don't need to read a book. You don't need to listen to another teaching or preaching CD or podcast. You don't need to memorise another Scripture. God uses willing vessels, not overflowing vessels. Throughout the Bible, in order to fulfil His plans on earth, God used many people from all walks of life:

God used Matthew—a government employee who became an apostle

God used Gideon—a common labourer who became a valiant leader of men

God used Deborah—a housewife who became a judge

God used Moses—a stutterer who became a deliverer

God used Jeremiah—a child who fearlessly spoke the word of God

God used Aaron—a servant who became God's spokesman

God used Nicodemus—a Pharisee who became a defender of the faith

God used David—a shepherd boy who became a king

God used Hosea—a marital failure who prophesied to save Israel

God used Joseph—a prisoner who became a Prime Minister

God used Esther—an orphan who became a queen

God used Elijah—a homely man who became a mighty prophet

God used Joshua—an assistant who became a conqueror

God used James and John—fishermen who became close disciples of Jesus, and were known as the Sons of Thunder

God used Abraham—a nomad who became a father of many nations

God used Jacob—a refugee and a deceiver who became the father of the twelve tribes of Israel

God used John the Baptist—a vagabond who became a forerunner of Jesus

God used Mary—an unknown virgin who gave birth to the Son of God

God used Nehemiah—a cupbearer who built the walls of Jerusalem

God used Shadrach, Meshach and Abednego—Hebrew exiles who became great leaders of Babylon
God used Hezekiah—son of an adulteress father who became the king renowned for doing right in the sight of God
God used Isaiah—a man of unclean lips who prophesied the birth of God's Messiah
God used Paul—a persecutor who became the greatest missionary in history and author of two thirds of the New Testament

Don't limit God, thinking He can't use you. At the end of the day, you are not doing it. You're just a willing vessel and God is doing it through you. You are the hands and feet of Jesus.

You may not be called to go overseas like I was, but God wants to use you in your place of work, home, community. That is your mission field. God has prepared people already that you can just go and connect to. Maybe they're sick, or in poverty, or dealing with a broken relationship, or in prison. They are crying out for somebody to come to them and you could be that person that would lead them to Jesus Christ.

During the Second World War, there was a poster of Sir Winston Churchill pointing, with the words: 'Britain needs you.' God is actually pointing to each and every one of us and saying: 'I need you. I need you in your workplace. I need you in the schools. I need you in your neighbourhood. I need you to speak out on behalf of Me. I need you as an ambassador. I need you as a minister of reconciliation in the communities around where you live.'

We need to give God permission to speak to us and have our ears open. Once we know that God wants the best for us, we can have complete peace when he speaks and not worry.

I've heard God's audible voice about 10 times in my life, but generally God communicates to us every day through His Holy Spirit and His Word. Sometimes people don't trust it or allow it. They may say 'praise God' and then go and make a cup of tea. The Holy Spirit has so much more to say to us! So, he waits until the next time.

The Holy Spirit gives us many opportunities. Sometimes we don't hear them, sometimes we say: 'You must be joking, I'm busy doing this or that.' But when you step out in willingness and obedience and tell the story, people say: 'Wow, I wish I could do that.' But they could if they chose to listen and obey!

For those of you who are married, I want to encourage you to pray for your partner. For those who are planning to get married, still pray for your partner. Pray that your partner will have the vision of God in their heart and mind. In other words, that is at the top of their priority list.

When God speaks to you it's important to write it down, because it's easy to get distracted sometimes. You can then go back to what you have heard and written and say: 'Lord, now I remember what you called us to do.' A few bullet points are sufficient. Include the main vision He's given you, whether it's preaching, caring for orphans, ministering to children, worshipping God through music, or serving in the marketplace. Be open and honest about your calling and any finances you need to fulfil it. Look for God to confirm your call. Again, if it's God plan, He will work out the details.

It is also important to share it with some trusted Christians who can advise, support and pray. Ministry can be lonely sometimes, but it's important to have a group of people behind you and believing in you. They are critical to success in ministry.

Jesus said: *'The thief comes only to steal and kill and destroy; I have come that they may have life and have it to the full.'* (John 10:10)

There's an amazing contrast between the devil's plan and God's plan. Jesus came to overcome the works of the devil and He was victorious in His job. And sometimes we need to remind the devil, ourselves and others that God has a good plan for your life—they are plans to prosper you and not to harm you (Jeremiah 29:11).

We hear voices from other people and from the enemy, but you can remind these voices of God's plan and purpose for your life.

He wants to use each and every one of us and His Word says He will strengthen those people. He will make you *'strong in the Lord and in the power of His might, with the full armour of God to take a stand against the devil's schemes.'* (Ephesians 6: 10,11)

In Luke 4 Jesus actually came to a point in His life that He recognized who He was, what His mission was and what His vision was. He spoke it out of His mouth with power and authority. Jesus knew the power of the tongue and the spoken Word. First of all, He comes against the devil with the rhema word (the spoken Word of of God) three times when he was tempted. I want to encourage you to speak something out of your mouth and say: 'It is written' just like Jesus. He declared it from His mouth in verse 18: *'The Spirit of the Sovereign Lord is on me, because He has anointed me to preach good news to the poor. He has sent me to proclaim freedom for the prisoners and recovery of sight for the blind, to release the oppressed, to proclaim the year of the Lord's favour.'* That statement is for you as well, to come to a point in your life that you recognize that the Spirit of God is on you, that the anointing is on you, that the boldness is on you, that the authority is on you to preach the good news. Wow! It makes it a whole lot easier.

You know sometimes before I preach and I speak, I have to speak this out to myself. I have to tell the devil, when he whispers in my ear: 'You can't preach! You can't teach! You're only Steve! You're Steve from Preston!' I have to declare the Word, that says: 'the spirit of the Sovereign Lord is on me and He has anointed me to preach the good news, to set the captives free!' You have to say it like you mean it. It has to come from your heart- a heart of compassion for people.

Get out there and do some damage to the devil's kingdom because the devil has got a hold on a lot of people. Whenever evangelist Lester Summral got off an aeroplane and entered a new place, he would say:

'Watch out, devil, I'm here!' And wherever I go, I say the same thing. I put the devil on notice that I am in that place to destroy his works. As you go and do what God has called you to do, know that you are victorious over all the works of the enemy.

And God has already prepared you and is still preparing you for a purpose. Preparation time is never wasted. Jesus spent 30 years of His life preparing for ministry.

Have confidence that as you put your faith and trust in God for what he has promised you and put on your heart for ministry, He will fulfil His promises. but you must carry out the plan. Sometimes people get side-tracked and start doing things God never called them to do. I did this and God had to direct me back to His path again!

We have a friend in Texas and the name of his ministry is No More Excuses. We can all do it- we're too young, too old, we don't know the Bible, we are too busy. But if we know that God's plan is for all men to be saved and we're part of that plan, we can't make excuses.

And don't tell God you can't. If God gives you something to do, remember that you can do all things through Christ. If you do your part in the natural, God will do His part in the supernatural. Rhema Bible Training Centre director Kenneth W. Hagin always told us: 'When you get the natural and the supernatural together, it is an explosive force for God.'

Too often people want the success they see others enjoy, but they don't want to pay the price it takes to have that success. There are costs associated with consecrating yourself to God. You may have to lay aside some desires and put them on the altar. You may even face disappointments and financial pressures. Know that there will be battles, problems, satanic attacks, oppression and even sickness. But praise God, by Jesus' stripes He has healed you and given you the victory in all areas of your life!

In Matthew 25:14-30 the master gave his three servants five talents, two talents and one talent. The one with five worked to double them to 10 and the one with two doubled them to make four. He didn't say to the one who had made the most: 'You've done better than him.' They had both doubled and did something with what had been given. And then he said: *'You've been faithful in the small things and I will give you more.'* You know God moves us on when we're faithful in the small things. He sees your faithfulness and then gives you more and moves you on to the next step in your life.

God is faithful to His promises and plan. He is a God who is worthy to be trusted. When God says something, we can depend on Him. He doesn't change His mind. He doesn't lie. He is consistent, constant and faithful. The Bible says in Lamentations 3:22-23, *'Through the Lord's mercies we are not consumed, because His compassions fail not. They are new every morning; Great is Your faithfulness.'*

All things are possible with God. We don't need to be afraid. God did not give us the spirit of fear, but the spirit of love, power and a sound mind (2 Timothy 1:7). If we can be led by the Spirit of God and not by our minds, then we can follow God's plan and see the results. We will be effective in what God is calling us to do.

Revelation 3:7-8 says, *'And to the angel of the church in Philadelphia write, "These things say He who is holy, He who is true, He who has the key of David, He who opens, no one shuts and shuts what no one opens. I know your works. See, I have set before you an open door, and no one can shut it; for you who have a little strength, have kept My word, and have not denied My name.'*

I pray that you catch His vision and live His dream for you. Just imagine how God will use you to make a difference in your own backyard or around the world. Hallelujah!

Prayer: Lord, thank you that you have an amazing plan for my life. Please help me to be open to your voice, to write down what you say to me, pray about it and then take action. Forgive me for the times that I have not acted on what you have told me. Help me to be obedient to your voice and give me the courage to step out of my comfort zone to fulfil your purposes for my life. I ask this in the name of Jesus. Amen

2
ALL THINGS ARE POSSIBLE FOR THOSE WHO BELIEVE

You have so much potential, but you will never reach fulfilment unless you use your faith. It connects us directly to fulfilling our potential. We get plugged into the supernatural realm of God's plan for our life by faith.

God loves taking ordinary people and turning them into extraordinary people of faith. If you're ordinary today, you're in the right place because God wants to do a mighty thing in your life.

Smith Wigglesworth was a normal man. He was a plumber who couldn't read or write until he was 22. In his ministry, he raised 25 people from the dead and had a vision for reaching 25 people for Jesus every single day and God honoured that. He stepped out in faith and God used him in a mighty way. He was known as the Apostle of Faith all over the world.

Hebrews 11:1 defines faith like this: *'Now faith is being sure of what we hope for and certain of the things we do not see.'*

'All things are possible for those who believe.' Is it possible that a Christian who has suffered poverty and debt all his life, to have his life turn around to prosperity? Is it possible for a Christian who has a physical illness for years to be healed? Is it possible that a Christian who has had a broken heart, can wake up one morning and be set free? Is it possible that somebody who has got pain and heaviness and has been plagued by a situation for years, can see it gone the next morning?

Jesus was making this qualifying statement that anything- all things, anything, everything- is possible for everyone, but it's only available for those who believe. Everybody has the potential to receive anything and everything from God, but it only moves to fulfilment by faith. In other words, you have to use your faith to believe to receive.

In Philippians 4:13 it says, *'I can do all things through Christ who strengthens me.'* Whatever it is that you've been believing God for, whatever you've been asking God for, whatever you've been dreaming about is possible. Why? Because all things and anything is possible for those who believe. It's possible to overcome that obstacle. It's possible to rise to the next level. It's possible to see your destiny come to pass in every area of your life. It's possible to move from potential to fulfilment by faith.

It's a bit like a staircase, when God leads you to take steps of faith. The bottom step is: 'I won't do it' or 'I can't do it', the next one is: 'I want to do it, how do I do it?' The next one up is: 'I'll try to do it.'

And then comes the recognition that 'I can do all things through Christ who strengthens me.' And then you can say: 'I can do it' and you have to take action and say: 'Ok, I will do it.' Then you are starting to move into fulfilment of the potential in you.

In Matthew 14:29, Jesus commanded Peter to step out of the boat. It was 3am, pitch black and the disciples were terrified. But Peter got out of the boat by faith on the command of Jesus, who said: 'Come.' He walked on water. And then he started to doubt. He looked at the circumstances and he started to sink.

I want you to get used to saying, 'I can,' rather than 'I can't.' I've had amazing opportunities to travel the world, helping people to discover an extraordinary life. That wouldn't have happened if we'd have stayed in the boat or on those bottom steps! A lot of people don't reach their fulfilment because they doubt, instead of believing. I encourage you to switch off your mobile phone and switch your faith on! A lot of people switch it on and off like a light switch.

When God told me to go out as a faith missionary, I did very little research so that I would go in faith and not start doubting. I've been a mechanical engineer for most of my life, from shop floor worker to director, so I'm a planner and an administrator. I do plan when I'm taking teams out on mission. I wouldn't expect people to jump into things that aren't organised. However, when you hear from God, you have a decision to make: 'Do I trust it or doubt it.' If we doubt it, we turn it into logic and reasoning which is the soul or natural realm. We start to say things like: 'I've only got £50 in the bank. I've got no holidays left. Who is going to look after the cat?' Eventually we talk ourselves out of it.

Some people get stuck in this area of unbelief and it's dangerous, because the Bible says you will receive when you believe. If you don't believe then you won't receive. That is dangerous for people who are in a poverty realm. That is dangerous for people who are sick. That's dangerous for people who are not saved.

In Mark 6:4 Jesus went to His own town: *'And Jesus said to them, "Only in His hometown amongst the relatives and His own house is a prophet without honour.'* He could not do any miracles there except lay

His hands on a few sick people and heal them. And He was amazed at their lack of faith.'

They missed the opportunity. They had the potential to be healed but because of their unbelief, Jesus couldn't do any miracles there.

In the Bible, there are 19 miracle stories and 12 people were healed because of their faith. People get saved because of their faith. People get healed because of their faith. People move to the next level because of their faith, so it's important that you don't get stuck in this area of doubt and unbelief because you will not receive.

Delete that unbelieving thought that is not according to the Word of God. The doubts come from the enemy, other people and our own words. Don't watch the replay. Switch it off! Fear opens the door to Satan but faith opens the door to God. You know the Bible tells us that God did not give us a spirit of fear, but of love, power, and a sound mind.

Did you know that the Bible tells us 365 times not to be afraid? That's one scripture for every day of the year! And do you know why we don't have to be afraid of anything? Because God is with us and He will never leave us nor forsake us!

Romans 12:2 says, *'Do not conform to the world any longer but be transformed by the renewing of your mind.'*

How do we renew our mind? With the Word of God and by putting it into action. And if you feed your faith, you will automatically starve your doubts.

We all received the measure of faith on the very day that we became born again. But it's up to us to do something with it. Faith won't move anything until it moves you. We need to give our faith a voice and verbalise it. We need to speak it out into the airwaves because it's powerful when we speak it out.

'He said: "I tell you the truth, if anyone says to this mountain go throw yourself into the sea and does not doubt in his heart but believes that what he says will happen it will done for him. Therefore, I tell you whatever you

ask for in prayer, believe that you've received it and it will be yours.'" (Mark 11:23)

Whatever you ask for, it's limitless. Open your mouth and be confident that God is our heavenly Father, we are His children, we are righteous, we can stand in His presence and ask by faith.

Every word you speak is a seed. Don't go and dig up your seed by speaking negatively and speaking unbelief and doubt. Water your seed. You know in Isaiah 61:3 it says: *'And they will be called oaks of righteousness, a planting of the Lord for the display of His splendour.'*

So how does faith come? Romans 10:17 says: *'Faith comes from hearing the message, and the message is heard through the word of Christ.'*

We also know that: *'Without faith it is impossible to please God'* (Hebrews 11:6).

Faith is based upon the knowledge of two things: the knowledge of who God is and the knowledge of what He has done. We do not have to pray for faith, fast for faith, or even try to get faith. God makes it available to every person who believes in Him.

Faith is like a muscle– everyone receives the same amount, but it is what you do with it that makes the difference. Some Christians get jealous because they see other Christians living better and experiencing more of the blessings of God in their lives. It is not because God loves them more. It's because they are exercising the faith that God gave them.

The measure of faith that every Christian receives can grow in two ways:

By feeding your faith on the Word of God.
In order for your physical body to grow or stay healthy, you need to feed your stomach with food. If you want your mind to grow, it needs knowledge. For faith to grow you need to feed your spirit with the Word of God. In Matthew 4:4, 'Jesus said: "It is written: 'Man does not live on bread alone, but on every word that comes from the

mouth of God.'" Our faith needs spiritual food to keep us alive and live a victorious Christian life.

Joshua 1:8 says: *'Do not let this Book of the Law depart from your mouth; meditate on it day and night, so that you may be careful to do everything written in it.'*

Meditation on God's Word is a method of feeding our spirits. As we meditate upon God's Word in an attitude of prayer, the Holy Spirit can give us revelation and illumination in our spirit, our faith will grow and we will mature as Christians.

By exercising it in your everyday life

It's up to you to do something with that measure of faith God gave you. It's up to you to put your faith into action and start living by faith. Every part of man- body, soul and spirit- can be developed. Our faith can grow. Feed your faith on the Word by hearing, reading, meditating and exercising your faith. Walk by faith and not by sight. Have faith in God. Let God be God. Expect great things from God as you attempt great things for God.

Seven Steps to the Highest Kind of Faith

1. **Know the Integrity of God's Word**
    The Bible is our number one textbook and 100% true. Hebrews 4:12 says, *'For the Word of God is living and active, sharper than any double-edged sword. It penetrates even to dividing soul and spirit, joints and marrow; it judges the thoughts and attitudes of the heart.'*
    God's Word will only come alive to you and work in your life as you accept it, act on it and walk in the light of it!

2. Know the Reality of Our Redemption in Christ

We are delivered from Satan's kingdom. We are now in God's Kingdom. Colossians 1:12-14 says: *'Giving thanks to the Father, who has qualified you to share in the inheritance of the saints in the Kingdom of Light. For He has rescued us from the dominion of darkness and brought us into the Kingdom of the Son He loves, in whom we have redemption, the forgiveness of sins.'* Jesus did it through His blood, by His death, burial and resurrection. We can't be in both kingdoms. We are either in the devil's kingdom or in God's family. Praise the Lord, He brought us out of the kingdom of darkness into the glorious Kingdom of Light!

We are also redeemed from sickness. It is God's will for us to be healed. God's Word tells us that we have authority over the devil through the blood of Jesus. This includes sickness and disease This was a revelation to me years ago and it changed my ministry.

'This was to fulfil what was spoken through the prophet Isaiah: "He took up our infirmities and carried our diseases.'" (Matthew 8:17). *'He Himself bore our sins in His body on the tree, so that we might die to sins and live for righteousness; by His wounds you have been healed.'* (1 Peter 2:24).

Our inheritance of deliverance and redemption from Satan is now. By faith you command the devil to remove himself from God's property! Our bodies are God's property and the devil has no right to enter it!

3. Know the Reality of the New Creation

The moment you accepted Jesus as your Lord and Saviour, you became new creations and the very life and nature of God himself entered your heart and spirit.

Stop looking at yourself from the natural standpoint. That will only bring defeat and give the devil a foothold. Start looking at yourself and others in the way God sees you.

Jesus paid the price and suffered for our sins. If we fall short, there is a way out. God has made a way! We can ask for forgiveness of our sins and God does not remember them any longer.

'If we confess our sins, He is faithful and just and will forgive us our sins and purify us from all unrighteousness.' (1 John 1:9)

'I, even I, am He who blots out your transgressions, for my own sake, and remembers your sins no more.' (Isaiah 43:25)

You are a new creature in Christ! The old really has gone and the new has come.

4. Know the Reality of Our Righteousness in Christ

We are made righteous o the very day we believed, and we have a good position, a right standing with God. A definition of righteousness is the ability to stand in God's presence without any sense of guilt, shame, condemnation or inferiority, as if we had never sinned. It was God who made us righteous through His Son when He made a perfect substitute for man.

'God made Him who had no sin to be sin for us, so that in Him we might become the righteousness of God.' (2 Corinthians 5:21)

Righteousness is a gift from God to all who believe in Jesus.

'But now righteousness from God, apart from the law, has been made known, to which the law and the prophets testify.' (Romans 3:21)

This righteousness from God comes through faith in Jesus Christ to all who believe. We can approach the throne with boldness every moment of every day without feeling condemned. We can enjoy the benefits and walk in the light of this knowledge.

5. **Know the Indwelling Presence of the Holy Spirit**
The Holy Spirit is the power source living in us. It's the same power that God used to raise Jesus from the dead. He will never leave us or forsake us.
'And His incomparably great power for us who believe. That power is like the working of His mighty strength, which he exerted in Christ when He raised Him from the dead and seated Him at His right hand in the heavenly realms.' (Ephesians 1:19–20)
'Now to Him who is able to do immeasurably more than all we ask or imagine, according to His power that is at work within us.' (Ephesians 3:20).
The Greater One living in us can make the impossible possible. The Holy Spirit is always a gentleman. He is the still small voice, the inner witness, the velvet feeling of peace on the inside of us. He is our Counsellor, Helper, Comforter, Teacher and the Spirit of truth living in us. We need to accept the indwelling presence of the Holy Spirit who works through us as we act in faith and be led by the Holy Spirit who tells us of things to come.

6. **Know the Reality of Our Fellowship with the Father**
'God, who has called you into fellowship with His Son Jesus Christ our Lord, is faithful.' (1 Corinthians 1:9)
We are called into fellowship with God and Jesus through prayer, praise, worship and thanksgiving. But we can't have fellowship without a relationship. In preparation for marriage

there is no relationship without dating, communicating and getting to know each other. Because of what Jesus has accomplished, we can have perfect fellowship with the Father anytime we want.

'I keep asking that the God of our Lord Jesus Christ, the glorious Father, may give you the spirit of wisdom and revelation so that you know Him better and I pray also that the eyes of your heart may be enlightened in order that you may know the hope to which He has called you, the riches of His glorious inheritance in the saints and His incomparable great power for us who believe.' (Ephesians 1:17)

7. **Know the Power and Authority We Have in the Name of Jesus**
   Jesus gave us the legal right to use His name and in John 14:13, John 14:14, John 15:16, and John 16:23, Jesus said whatever you ask the Father in My name, it will be given. It's important to pray to the Father in the name of Jesus, because authority and power is released in His name. The name of Jesus is above all names and every knee shall bow to it and every tongue confess that He is Lord. Too often we pray in Jesus' name out of habit. But we need to understand that when we use the name of Jesus, we release power and authority in heaven, on earth and under the earth.

I encourage you to rise up, step out and step up to a higher level of faith. Recognise the realities of what God has done for us by sending Jesus. Enjoy your inheritance of what rightfully belongs to you in Christ. As you accept these redemptive realities in your life, it will help you live a victorious life in Christ– a life full of the highest kind of faith. All things are possible for those who believe.

Prayer: Father, please help me to increase my faith by reading and meditating on Your truths and walking by faith and not by sight. Help me in my unbelief and give me the courage to take the next steps and change 'I can't' into 'I can'. I ask this in the name of Jesus. Amen

3
GO AND MAKE DISCIPLES
OF ALL NATIONS

There are 7.7 billion people on earth and God sent Jesus to die for every one of them. God's plan is about all people. John 3:16 says: *'For God so loved the world that He gave His only begotten Son, that whoever believes in Him will not perish but have everlasting life.'*

God didn't send Jesus for a select group of people. No, He sent Jesus for all people and He wants all of them to be saved. And we all have a part to play in 'The Great Commission', as commanded by Jesus in Matthew 28: 19-20.

'All authority in heaven and on earth has been given to me. Therefore, go and make disciples of all nations, baptizing them in the name of the Father and of the Son and of the Holy Spirit, and teaching them to obey everything I have commanded you. And surely, I am with you always, to the very end of the age.'

Evangelism is the completion of the fulfilment of the Great Commission of reconciling man back to God. An evangelist is someone verbally communicating or proclaiming the gospel on behalf of God and disclosing the revelation of Jesus Christ to others, so that they can be saved and receive all the benefits.

Some people are specifically called by God to be apostles, evangelists, teachers or pastors, to prepare God's people for works of service (Ephesians 4:11-14). But the Great Commission is a calling for all believers. It's not just the pastor's job to evangelise. It's a bit like a football team that has a great coach. The coach shows them videos, trains them in moves, ensure they eat the right food. But on the day of the match the coach is not on the football field. It's the players who have to go out and play the game and score goals. The pastor's job is to teach, train, equip and prepare believers and then kick us out, saying: 'Go and do some damage to the devil's kingdom!'

Currently more than 60 million people have heard the gospel. Nearly 21 million people become Christians and 50,000 new churches are planted every year. But only 30% of the world is actually saved. Nations are waiting. There is a harvest of people waiting right now for someone to step out in faith and speak out on behalf of God, as an ambassador, a diplomat and a mouthpiece for the Kingdom of God.

Romans 10:14 says, *'How then shall they call on Him in whom they have not believed? And how shall they believe in Him of whom they have not heard? And how shall they hear without a preacher?'*

There are people out there in the world that have never heard the name of Jesus. The Bible says that when this Gospel is preached as a testimony to all nations, then the end will come. In the meantime, we have a job to do before Jesus returns. We need to get involved with spreading the gospel. But there is an urgency for people to believe in Jesus because we don't know when He is coming back. If He came back right now, the people who are unbelievers would go to hell.

God is not condemning people to hell. People are going to hell because they have not believed. It sounds like a hard statement, but it's according to the word of God (Mark 16:16, John 3:17). They're making their own choices and it's our responsibility to tell them about Jesus to prevent them from going to hell. And the Bible says when you believe you will receive. When people believe, they receive healing. When people believe, they are set free from demonic spirits. When people believe, they receive the full benefits package of salvation.

We have seen that God wants us to arise, so the people can see Him. Our country and world belongs to God, but the devil keeps a lot of people blinded in their minds and hearts so they cannot see the true living God! In Exodus 5:1 Moses tells Pharaoh to *'let my people go.'* We can proclaim that the devil must let the people go because every man was created by God. Everyone belongs to Him.

God wants His kingdom full. He doesn't want it half full, but full to the top! Evangelist Reinhard Bonnke once said: 'We should plunder hell to populate heaven. God wants to move everybody from the kingdom of darkness to the kingdom of light.

There's a banquet in heaven. Everybody's invited to the banquet, but they have to believe. And you have to tell them.

Jesus said: *'The harvest truly is plentiful.'* A harvest almost beyond measure or beyond our imagination. It is exciting to go out there and get people saved and filled with the Holy Spirit, discipling them to become spiritually mature. What a privilege it is to be a labourer together with God. What an honour it is to be an ambassador of God in the world. We are speaking on behalf of God, the maker of heaven and earth. Hallelujah!

Many people rise up out of their poverty just because they hear that God has a good plan for their lives and they've been redeemed from the curse of the law. It's such a blessing to go into poor parts of the world and to see them prosper just because they hear the good news that God is a good God, He loves them and has a plan for them. That plan is to prosper them and not to harm them, a plan to give them a hope and a future (Jeremiah 29:11). He's a caring God. He's a passionate God. He loves his creation and He wants to see them succeed. He wants the best for their life.

You know, angels don't preach the gospel. Muslims don't preach the gospel. Hindus don't preach the gospel. We are the preachers! We're the marketing people for God so that His plan can be fulfilled.

And there is such rejoicing in heaven when someone is saved! I have an African friend called Emmanuel, who tells the story of how he died during the atrocities in Rwanda in the 90's and came back to life. He had a vision that Jesus took him on a tour of heaven and he saw angels with golden guitars. And every time one person on earth gave their life to Jesus Christ then the angels played their golden guitars.

He also told me that he was on an aeroplane in Africa, when one of the engines caught fire and smoke started filling the cabin. People were panicking and crying, but he stood up and preached the gospel. They all got saved. The flames went out, the smoke disappeared and the flight carried on as normal!

Another pastor I know, Bill Henderson, preached the gospel on planes for 20 years before 9/11 and many people got saved. God can give us so many opportunities if we are willing!

The Bible tells us that we're ambassadors for Christ. We're speaking out on behalf of God and we need to be joyful about that. We have good news to share with people- a message that will change their life forever. But we've got to remember that we're approaching people who are not spiritual. Sometimes we need to be normal with people in terms of evangelism and people will receive it.

We are the generation. We are the ones who have the responsibility. And we've got every single opportunity and tool and resources that we need to get the gospel to this world. But part of our problem is our mouth- we have a zip on it. Some people also have a padlock and they've thrown away the key!

Fear comes from the devil. Fear is not from God. The devil will do everything that he can to keep your mouth closed. What do you fear when telling somebody about Jesus? That they might spit at you? That they might swear at you? That they might smack you? They might do. I haven't heard of many people who've been killed for telling somebody that God loves them. What's the worst thing that could happen? They might not speak to you again. But what is the best thing that could happen? They might just say: 'Can you lead me to the Lord? Can you pray for me?'

God wants all men to be saved, baptised in the Holy Spirit and grow up spiritually. He doesn't want us to stay spiritual babies all our life. Babies are cute. But if you see a 21-year-old person still wearing a nappy, with a milk bottle in their pocket and a dummy in their mouth, it would be kind of sad. God wants us to grow up and mature into those full-grown, mature and victorious Christians who will be committed and obedient to God's plan for this earth.

Your local area is a good place to start. If you've got a map of your area and you start looking at that, I guarantee God will speak to you and guide you where to go and who to speak to.

Hospitals are a great place to minister. If you don't know where to go, go to the hospital and pray for somebody who is sick. Maybe they will be healed or give their lives to Jesus. They might even get baptized in the Holy Spirit.

But wherever you go, think about this question: Why should anybody hear the gospel twice when some people haven't heard it once? If I fish, I can spend a lot of time fishing in a lake and not catch anything. But why should I stay there? I need to go to a place teeming with fish. It's the same with people. Sometimes we keep preaching the gospel to the same group of people and it's hard work sometimes. So, go and preach somewhere else.

The Bible says that Apollos watered and Paul planted the seed. We've got to plant and water the seed, but sometimes there's new ground that we need to plant the seed in. The new ground is made of people who haven't heard about Jesus in areas where Christianity is not very prevalent. I believe that's where we need to put our faith into action, step out and preach the Word as Jesus told us.

Smith Wigglesworth, the great English apostle of faith had many different stories of raising people from the dead and healing sickness. But one thing that he had was an evangelistic heart. He used to pray and believe God every day that 25 people would give their life to Jesus. But you can start much smaller than that, such as committing to leading at least one person per year to Jesus Christ. Just ask God to give you opportunities to tell people about Jesus.

Paul said this in Ephesians 6:19: *'Pray also for me that whenever I open my mouth words will be given me so that I will fearlessly make known the mystery of the gospel.'* We're talking about this great apostle Paul, and he's saying: *'Pray for me, please.'*

We don't have to think about what we're going to say or write it down on paper and worry about it. No! We just have to open our mouth by faith as we are led by the Holy Spirit in what to say! It's powerful stuff. It's powerful when we open our mouth and we talk about God to people. Something happens in their spirit, because everybody on this earth knows God somewhere in their heart.

Jesus taught His disciples to be fishers of men. And there's a whole range of fishing techniques! We can preach by speaking the Word, by putting love into action or by a simple smile. Food is also a great communicator. People talk and open up over food, so that's a great way to get to know people and form a relationship with them. It might cost you a bit of money to invite people out for coffee and cakes and meals, but God will reward you for that. We need to look at God's vision and not the circumstances. The foundation of a successful ministry is not money, it's a heart and a compassion for people.

There are so many creative ways to reach people with the gospel and in the past I've encouraged people to run aerobics classes, meetings in McDonalds, cookery classes- my late wife Detty was saved after being invited to a Chinese cooking class!

Don't get too focused just on one technique. Be creative, because the good news is that there's plenty of fish in the sea. If one method doesn't work, try another. You might start to get a few bites. But I believe that one of the most effective ways is one-to-one evangelism and building relationships with people you come into contact with daily. You'll never know who you might meet. Somebody might just ask you to pray for them. Do everything with love and compassion, pouring love into action.

Like Jesus, we have to go out and meet the people. Jesus went about the villages teaching and preaching and healing the sick. He saw the crowd and he had compassion, He saw that in His mind and with His physical eyes, but also with His spiritual eyes. He had compassion for people.

Keep it simple. Don't complicate the gospel. You don't have to show people the whole Bible before they say yes. There's time for that later.

A question you could ask people is: 'If you were to die today, would you be sure and confident that you're going to heaven?' A lot of people will answer: 'I'm not sure. Maybe. If God's in a good mood and if I'm a good boy (or girl) that day and if I've done some good works, maybe I'll go to heaven. Maybe I'll make it.' That gives you an opportunity to talk about your assurance through Jesus.

I encourage you to use God's Word, because it's powerful and it's active, like a double-edged sword. You never know how you can change people's lives by speaking just one scripture. Don't be frightened of using it. Praise God, until now we have not been put in prison! The police have never come knocking on my door because of it.

Meditate on Philippians 4:4-6, which says: *'Rejoice in the Lord always. Again, I will say, rejoice! Let your gentleness be known to all men.*

The Lord is at hand. Be anxious for nothing, but in everything by prayer and supplication, with thanksgiving, let your requests be made known to God.'

1 John 5:14-15 is also an important scripture to remember: *'Now this is the confidence that we have in Him, that if we ask anything according to His will, He hears us. And if we know that He hears us, whatever we ask, we know that we have the petitions that we have asked of Him.'*

Don't be offended when people say things against what you believe, because our responsibility is to speak out on behalf of God, isn't it? Our responsibility is to preach the gospel fearlessly and not be too worried about that. You don't have to strangle them until they got purple in the face, saying: 'You accept Jesus now or I'll choke you!' Just tell them God loves them. And God will give you opportunities to do that if He knows you're willing.

You certainly need to tell your own family that God loves them, but it might not be your task to lead your family members to the Lord. That task could belong to someone else, so pray for laborers to go into your family to share the good news.

We do our best and God will do the rest. When the Holy Spirit speaks through us, it's a voice of power and authority and people receive that. Some people reject that, but this is their choice. But praise God, he has given us many opportunities to fearlessly make known the mystery of the gospel.

There are not many things that are free, but that benefits package of the gospel is free and you have it in your hand. You have the key to their door to unlock the mystery of the gospel for them. It's your responsibility. It's a tough one because it's not always easy to do something that we've never done before. But I tell you, when you lead somebody to Jesus, there is such a joy that comes when you know that the devil has lost his grip on them and they're going to heaven. Hallelujah!

Prayer: Father, please me opportunities and situations to tell people that God loves them and Jesus died for them. Enable me to build relationships and speak your Word into their lives, to pray for them and lead them in the prayer of salvation. Give me the words to speak and the boldness to speak them, in the name of Jesus. Amen

4

STORE UP FOR YOURSELVES TREASURES IN HEAVEN

A pastor had a vision for a new building. Over several months he shared with the congregation the Scriptural confirmation, blueprints, timescale and cost. Everyone was excited about this new project. One Sunday, he announced: 'I've got some good news and some bad news for you! The good news is that we have the money!' Everybody was excited. The praise and worship team went faster, people were dancing and hugging each other and saying: 'Praise the Lord! God is so good! God is our Provider!' After about 10 minutes the pastor said: 'Calm down. I want to tell you the bad news.' So, they all looked at each other and said: 'How can there be bad news when we've got the money?'
'The bad news is that the money is in your pocket!'

The gospel is free, but it takes money to preach it. Money is needed to supply things for literature, crusades, transport, sound equipment, lighting, musicians, revival meetings, buildings, orphanages, children's support, hospitals, prison ministry, etc.

Don't be tight-fisted with your money when it comes to the gospel. We have the money- it's in our pockets and banks accounts and all we have to do is release it. We have enough resources to get the gospel to the ends of the world, and yet we still find excuses not to give it. Release it into the kingdom of God and you will see that as you sow your seed into good ground, it will produce fruit- a harvest beyond measure.

I have another story for you. Three days before a very rich guy was about to die, he told his wife his last wish: 'Go to each of my bank accounts and draw out the money in cash. Before they close my coffin lid, put all my money inside the coffin with me.'

She said: 'I can't do that!'

'Come on, you're a good Christian lady and this is my last request. It's all I want. Please honour my request.'

Finally, she agreed and told a friend about her ailing husband's request. He died and at the funeral, the coffin was there with all the flowers on it. When the widow's friend suddenly remembered the man's final wish, she asked: 'Did you do what he wanted you to do?'

'Yes. I went to all his bank accounts, got all his ATM cards and bank books and drew out all the cash and put it into my bank account. Then I wrote him out a cheque and put it in the coffin.'

As much as you like, you can't take your money with you when you die. On the day you stand before God, you'll be the same as everyone else- naked and bare. You won't have your credit card, bank account, cars or houses.

However, you can do something with it while you're here on earth. You can make a difference by extending God's kingdom. But you'll have to be willing to release the money from your pockets and bank accounts.

The world is full of things that seem to shout: 'Buy me! Buy me! Buy me!' The temptation is to fill your house with goods and wardrobes with clothes. Many conversations revolve around money. Everyone likes spending it, but does anyone like giving money away?

Jesus said it's more blessed to give than to receive. I've reached a stage in my life where it's such a joy to give. But it wasn't always the case. I would sit in church with my hands in my pockets and rationalise by saying: 'These preachers only want money to build big buildings.' My giving was sort of like a story my dad used about church offerings during Christmas. He would say that if you shook the offering bag, all you could hear was noise from all the coins inside.

The Bible says in John 8:32: *'When you know the truth, the truth will set you free.'* The church must be set free in this area of money. I hear some people say: 'Well, I can't go anywhere because I've got a big debt. When my bank account gets up to a certain limit, then I'll go into the ministry or on the mission field.' That's not faith! Faith believes the finances will come in to fulfil God's plan as you go. You must walk by faith, not by sight, rather than wait until you can see the money in your account.

What are you doing with your money anyway? 1 Timothy 6:10 says: *'For the love of money is the root of all kinds of evil.'* Many people love money and are eager to get more and spend more.

Someone I know who got promoted in their job told me he still never had any money, despite having more if it! Most people are in debt because of their wants, not because of their needs. I see it therefore I want it. It's an epidemic!

You must control your desires. You can't allow your 'wants' to consume all your money. The Bible says in Matthew 6:24: *'No one can serve two masters, either he will hate the one and love the other, or he will be devoted to the one and despise the other. You cannot serve both God and money.'*

Hebrew 13:5 warns: *'Keep your lives free from the love of money and be content with what you have because God has said: "Never will I leave you and never will I forsake you."'*

Myths about money may cause you to think wrongly about it. And there are lots of promises that money offers. Don't believe any of them:

False promise number one. Happiness comes with more possessions. Perhaps you believe that the more money you have, the happier you'll become. Jesus said in Luke 12:15: 'Watch out, be on your guard against all kinds of greed. A man's life does not consist in the abundance of his possessions.'

False promise number two. Importance comes with more possessions. People think the bigger their speedboat, the bigger their car, the bigger their house, the more important they become. It's not true. Ecclesiastes 5:10 says: 'Whoever loves money never has enough money.'

False promise number three. Security comes in having more possessions. Proverbs 11:28 says: 'He who trust in his riches will fall but the righteous will flourish like foliage.' Proverbs 18:18: 'The rich man thinks of his wealth as an impregnable defence, as a high wall of safety.' What a dreamer!

James 1:5 tells you how to handle money wisely: *'If any of you lacks wisdom, let him ask of God, who gives to all liberally and without reproach, and it will be given to him.'*

Reject the false promise that happiness comes in having more possessions!

Reject the false promise that importance comes in having more possessions!

Reject the false promise that security comes in having more possessions!

There is no need to rely on money for security. If you follow God's plan, He will provide for it. There's no doubt about it. When you step out in faith, God will provide everything that you need.

Ask yourself what you're doing with your money. I believe that God is going to ask you some important questions when you pass away from this earth, such as: 'What did you do with the resources I gave you? What did you do with the money that I put into your possession? Were you a good steward of it? What did you spend the money on? Did you spend it on yourself? Or did you spend it on advancing the kingdom of God on this earth?' Are you ready to answer?

Realizing that I must be accountable for the money entrusted in my care, encourages me to think differently about.

God will give you wisdom on how to release our money into His kingdom business. If you pray specifically and strategically, saying: 'Father how do you want me to release this money? Where do you want me to release this money, that you put me in charge of?'

Don't forget that God gives you every bit of the money you have, but he only asks for 10% as a tithe. That leaves you with 90 percent to decide what to do with. If you remain open to hear from the Holy Spirit about what to do with your money, you will see something different happening in your life. I can testify that God blesses in areas of finances.

Don't think that because you don't have a lot of money that you can't give to mission. Giving from your heart is what's important. Some people have said to me: 'I can't afford to give to missions because I can only give £10 per month.' I say: 'Praise the Lord. That's a lot of money.' Imagine if you've got a hundred people giving £10 a month, that's £1000. It's not about the amount. Never think your bit won't count. That money is like a seed that you're planting. You're giving somebody an opportunity to preach the gospel and go places where people have never been.

And remember to increase your giving as God blesses you financially! There was a man who went to his pastor and said: 'Pastor, I'd like to talk to you about tithing. Ten years ago, I used to earn £100 per month and it was easy to tithe. I could just give my £10. Now God has blessed me so much I earn £1,000,000 per month. I find it difficult to tithe now. I need to give £100,000 every month. Please pray for me.'

The pastor was very quiet and the man eventually said: 'Pastor, are you not going to pray for me?'

He responded: 'I'm just trying to get the right words to ask God to put you back on the salary that you used to be on so that it's easy to tithe.'

Money can either prevent the gospel from going out or help it advance. Jesus tells us to *'go into all the world and preach the Good News; make disciples of all nations.'* And when you go, you shouldn't worry about money. Jesus didn't say: 'when your bank account is full.' The only thing that He said is to go with the power of the Holy Spirit and preach the gospel. As long as the Holy Spirit leads you, guides you and teaches you, the money will flow.

The kingdom of God can only be established on earth by people who have kingdom-driven lives, who have a kingdom mentality, sensitive and obedient to His plans, purposes and desires for the lost. If you are going to reach people, then think of ways to get practically, prayerfully and financially involved with God's plan. Malachi 3:6 warns against robbing God, but as you sow your seed, you can expect a harvest.

John 10:10 tells us that, *'the enemy comes to kill, steal and destroy, but Jesus came so that we might have life and have it more abundantly.'* Hallelujah! It is God's plan that you prosper, but you've got to trust Him. God is the source of your finances and your prosperity.

There is no need to pressure people about giving and talk about it all the time. Trust that as you participate in His plan, He will provide all the resources and finances needed to get the job done. Whatever He asks you to do is His project anyway, not your own. Malachi says: *'Don't rob God... test me...'* I encourage you and even I challenge you to give. I believe you will see the windows of heaven open wide. God is a good God. Simply sow your seed on good ground in obedience to Him.

If you have a ministry and you expect others to support it, then willingly sow your personal finances into other ministries. Why should you expect other people to release finances into your ministry at home or on the mission field, if you don't release your tithes and offerings? So, I encourage you to be faithful in sowing your seed and have faith in God. I believe that sowing finances is one of the keys to success in ministry. Give out of a love for God and people. I encourage you to step up to a higher level and have faith in God.

I've seen it in my life so many times. I not boasting about what I give, but I'm only sharing to boost your faith. I have given people houses, motorbikes, food and shelter. It's just as exciting to give as it is to see how God returns the blessing some ten, thirty and a hundredfold, just like the Bible says.

And remember, if you need money to do what God is telling you to do, let people know and give them an opportunity to get involved. If I had never sent emails to my friends and supporters, they would have never been able to release the money God had told them to give. Perhaps they would have doubted if God had spoken to them at all. Give people an opportunity to give because as they give, it will be given back to them, pressed down, shaken together and running over. If we don't give people that opportunity, then we just may prevent them from receiving the blessings of giving.

Some people are called to go, while others are called to stay and support ministers and missionaries. So, everyone has a role to fulfil in God's plan. Try it, trust God and sow seeds into His ministry and watch the blessings return to you!

Prayer: Father, I recognise that my money is a gift from you. Enable me to put you first in every area of my finances and to trust you to provide for my needs. Enable me to sow into Your kingdom business in increasing measure and receive your abundant blessings in my life as a result. I ask this in the name of Jesus. Amen

5
WHATEVER YOU ASK
IN MY NAME

Prayer is always going to be supernatural because of the divine One living inside of you. Prayer changes things. As you pray, make room for the supernatural by yielding to the Holy Spirit and responding to Him. When we do, limits are removed off God that we have placed on Him, causing us to go further and higher with God.

The disciples asked Jesus in Luke 11:1: *'Lord, teach us to pray.'* And Jesus gave them a model prayer in Matthew 6:5-14, known as 'The Lord's Prayer'. It is a prayer pattern in which we see certain principles of prayer:

'And when you pray, do not be like the hypocrites, for they love to pray standing in the synagogues and on the street corners to be seen by men. I tell you the truth, they have received their reward in full. But when you pray, go into your room, close the door and pray to your Father, who is unseen. Then your Father, who sees what is done in secret, will reward you. And when you pray, do not keep on babbling like pagans, for they think they will be heard because of their many words. Do not be like them, for your Father knows what you need before you ask him. This, then, is how you should

pray: Our Father in heaven, hallowed be your name, your kingdom come, your will be done on earth as it is in heaven. Give us today our daily bread. Forgive us our debts, as we also have forgiven our debtors. And lead us not into temptation but deliver us from the evil one. For if you forgive men when they sin against you, your heavenly Father will also forgive you. (Matthew 6:5-14)

Jesus tells us about principles of private prayer and how we should not be like the hypocrites and not babbling like pagans. He was saying: 'Be careful that we do not pray to be seen by men.'

Private prayer is very important. We should not just be praying when crisis hit us. We should be spiritually prepared for those moments through our daily private prayer time.

Jesus talks about principle of repetitious prayer and says that heathens pray like this, hoping to be heard by their gods. Sometimes Christians act like those heathens when they pray, thinking that God will hear them because of their lengthy and repeated prayer. God knows what we need before we ask, yet He still wants us to ask. He is not just going to hear you because you pray very loud or very long.

Jesus taught His disciples some basic principles of prayer. Jesus was not telling the disciples to pray this prayer word for word every time they pray. He gave them some principles of prayer, that work for the church today.

Jesus talks about the principles of putting God first. If we put God first in our lives, in all areas, then we do not have to worry. He will provide for us.

Jesus teaches us the principle of daily prayer and the importance of asking God daily for our every need.

He also talks about the principle of forgiveness, one of the essential elements of prayer. Don't expect results in your prayer life if you have unforgiveness in your heart.

Doctors have long discovered if people have unforgiveness or bitterness in their hearts, they are more susceptible to certain types of diseases. Our inner feelings are very closely related to our physical health! If you forgive, you have to forget also, just as God forgives and chooses to forget our sin.

In Matthew 7:7-11 Jesus teaches again on prayer, telling us to ask, seek and knock. We need to keep on believing and pray the prayer of faith. It is not the prayer of unbelief that brings results.

There is power when we pray in accordance to the principles laid down by Jesus- in unity about the same thing, in the same direction, in harmony, in one accord, in one mind, one heart, one voice, and one spirit. When we pray together in unity, the power of God is released and the anointing flows, greater works can be done in more places, more healing, more salvation.

So, be specific and strategic in your prayers. Proverbs 16:3 says: *'Commit to the Lord whatever you do, and your plans will succeed.'* It is important to notice what this scripture doesn't say. It doesn't say your plans might succeed or could succeed. If you pray a prayer of consecration like Jesus prayed: *'Not my will, Father, but your will be done.'* I guarantee God will answer you. Sometimes I believe that too much time in prayer is spent spewing hot air and uttering useless words. Rather than being direct and specific with our prayers, we can talk all around the subject. That is not necessary. God answers prayers according to His will, not our vain babble.

Above all, pray in the Father's will. If you're praying for the lost, you know He will answer because His will on earth is that all men be saved and be Spirit-filled and that all men grow, develop, mature and go out and make disciples. So, you can expect God to answer your prayers.

The Six Most Important Things about Prayer.

1. Pray to the Father in Jesus' name. Too often we pray in Jesus' name out of a habit. The phrase 'in Jesus' name' is the power in our prayers. It's the power of attorney or the right to use His name. In John 14:13-14, John 15:16, John 16:23-24 the phrase *'whatever you ask in My name'* is repeated. The key to success is to address our prayers and approach the Father in Jesus' name. The name of Jesus is above all names- in heaven and on earth and under the earth. Every knee shall bow at the name of Jesus. There is authority in the name of Jesus, and when we pray in Jesus' name, we exercise this authority. Knowing the authority that you have in His name is to know your legal rights in Christ. Praying in the name of Jesus is the key to answered prayer - the key that opens doors which gives power to our prayers.

2. Believe and you will receive. The Bible tells us in Mark 11:24, 'Therefore I tell you, whatever you ask for in prayer, believe that you have received it, and it will be yours.' God will do anything for those who have faith in Him. The Bible says 'believe' not 'hope.' We are saved by grace through faith. It is the prayer of faith that God listens to and we will receive when we pray in faith. You have to believe first. Many people want to receive first, it is always the believing part first! Many people pray in unbelief. They ask again and again in prayer for the same thing, but if they would believe that when they pray, then receive and thank God, they would not ask again. We ought to believe in our heart, even though we do not see.

3. Forgive when you pray. *'And when you stand praying, if you hold anything against anyone, forgive him, so that your Father in heaven may forgive you your sins.'* (Mark 11:25-26) Before we can expect an answer to our prayers, we must forgive those who have wronged us. Prayer does not work in an unforgiving and bitter heart. You are responsible for your life not for somebody else's life. Whatever is in somebody else's heart can't hinder your prayer, but what you have against another person can hinder your prayers. The root of bitterness and envy in our heart and mind will wreck our spiritual life. So, forgive when you pray.

4. Depend upon the Holy Spirit in your prayer life. *'And pray in the Spirit on all occasions with all kinds of prayers and requests.'* (Ephesians 6:18) When we allow the Holy Spirit to pray through us and help us in our prayer life, we will see amazing answers to our prayers. Our nation needs prayer, the church and we as individuals need prayer. Many Christians pray with their understanding, but not many pray with the Spirit, in tongues. Many don't even know it is possible, or because of ignorance of scripture, they believe that it is done away with. But what belonged to the Corinthian church still belongs to us today. Paul says when he prayed in an unknown tongue, his spirit prayed. When you pray in tongues, it is your spirit praying by the Holy Spirit within you which gives you the utterance.

5. Pray the prayer of intercession. *'In the same way, the Spirit helps us in our weakness. We do not know what we ought to pray for, but the Spirit himself intercedes for us with groans that words cannot express.'* (Romans 8:26). The prayer of intercession is not for you. An intercessor is one who takes the place for another. Every spirit-filled believer can expect the Holy Spirit to help him when praying or interceding for somebody else, even for people we don't know, because the Holy Spirit knows him.

6. **Edify yourself by praying in the Holy Spirit.** This is a time when we are not praying for someone else, but purely a time of personal spiritual edification. *'But you, dear friends, build yourselves up in your most holy faith and pray in the Holy Spirit.'* (Jude 20) It is a time when we build, charge and edify ourselves. We all need this kind of prayer. It is a means of spiritual edification, praying for things which we know nothing about and building up our faith.

As well as prayer, the Bible teaches us about the importance of fasting. In Matthew 6:16-18, we read: *'When you fast, do not look sombre as the hypocrites do, for they disfigure their faces to show others they are fasting. Truly I tell you, they have received their reward in full. But when you fast, put oil on your head and wash your face, so that it will not be obvious to others that you are fasting, but only to your Father, who is unseen; and your Father, who sees what is done in secret, will reward you'.*

In most cases fasting is a private matter between the individual and God. However, we can have occasional times of cooperate or public fast (Joel 2:15; Acts 14:23). The corporate fast of a church can be a wonderful and powerful experience, provided that the people are in harmony and unity in these matters. Problems in the church can be dealt with and relationships can be healed through unified prayer and fasting. It can also be a time of refreshment and personal revival. Throughout Scripture fasting refers to abstaining from food for spiritual purpose only. You are free to fast however the Spirit leads you.

In Scripture the normal means of fasting involves a total fast-abstaining from all foods, but not from water. In the forty day fast of Jesus, we are told that *'He ate nothing'* and that toward the end of the fast *'He was hungry.'* Satan tempted Him to eat, indicating that the abstaining was from food, but not from water (Luke 4:2).

Sometimes what could be considered a partial fast is described, which is a restriction of diet but not total abstention. *'I ate no delicacies; no meat or wine entered my mouth'* (Daniel 10:3). There are also several examples in Scripture of what has been called an 'absolute fast' which is abstaining from food and water (Esther 4:16). Paul engaged in such fast following his encounter with the living Christ (Acts 9:9).

It must be understood that the absolute fast is the exception and should never be engaged in unless one has a very clear command from God.

Fasting must always centre on God. If our fasting is not unto God, we have failed. Physical benefits, success in prayer, the enduing with power, spiritual insights– these must never replace God as the centre of our fasting. Once the primary purpose of fasting is firmly fixed in our hearts, we are at liberty that there are also secondary purposes in fasting.

'I humbled my soul with fasting' (Psalm 69:10). Anger, bitterness, jealousy, strife, fear– if they are within us, they will surface during fasting. We can rejoice in this knowledge, because we know that healing is available through the power of Christ.

Be alert! Besides fasting from food, you can also fast from things that distract, such as TV, the internet, mobile phones, computer games or things that destroy such as coarse jesting or careless words. In all this we can expect God to reward those who diligently seek Him.

Set aside time each day to seek God in prayer and fasting. As with all the disciplines, a progression should be observed. You may begin with a partial fast and abstain from solid food for an extended part of the day. Fresh fruit juices are excellent to drink during a fast. Outwardly you will be performing the regular duties of the day, but inwardly you will be experiencing a greater awareness of prayer and adoration, song, and worship. Break your fast with a light meal (avoiding chilly or acidic foods if possible) or fresh fruits and vegetables and a good deal of inner rejoicing.

In conclusion, by asking, seeking and knocking in faith, we can enjoy the abundant blessings God has for His children. Prayer is about believing and receiving by faith. As you pray, trust God and make room for the supernatural to flow by yielding and responding to the Holy Spirit.

Remember, above all, there is no limit in your prayer life. Jesus says: 'Whatever you ask.' No limitation!

Prayer: Lord, please deepen and strengthen my prayer life so that I can pray bold prayers of faith; prayers that release your miraculous Holy Spirit power into a lost and dying world. Help me to pray in every circumstance, *'by prayer and petition, with thanksgiving'* and avoid the traps of unbelief, mindless repetition and unforgiveness. I ask this in the power and authority of Jesus, the Name above every name. Amen

6
I WILL BUILD MY CHURCH

God's plan is that all men be saved and filled with the Holy Spirit, which gives us supernatural power to change a community. Jesus said: *'And you will be my witness. And you will receive power when the Holy Spirit comes on you.'*

John 14:16-17 says: *'And I will pray the Father, and He will give you another Helper, that He may abide with you forever, the Spirit of truth, whom the world cannot receive, because it neither sees Him nor knows Him; but you know Him, for He dwells with you and will be in you.'* Jesus was teaching His disciples that when it was time for Him to go to His Father, He would not leave them alone. He promised to send them Someone who would enable them to walk in the same light and power that He walked in.

The apostles used that mighty power on the day of Pentecost- 120 of them. Among them was Mary the mother of Jesus Christ. She spoke in tongues too. Once you're born again, then you've got the qualification to be baptized in the Holy Spirit and receive the supernatural power to become a witness for Jesus.

I just love reading the book of Acts. Here we have Peter, who denied Jesus three times when He was going to the cross. When Peter gets filled with the Holy Spirit, he stood up before the crowds and said: 'You are the ones who killed the Son of God.' And they were cut to their heart and 3,000 people got saved that day. Later he heals a man crippled from birth by using that supernatural power.

The Holy Spirit is available for every single person who believes. Don't hold back because the biggest purpose for the baptism of the Holy Spirit is not just so that we can speak with tongues or have a wonderful experience. It's to give us the power that we need to be a witness for Jesus.

The secret to success is to get started and don't quit. If you've never laid hands on people to receive healing, it's time you started. If you've never led somebody to be baptized in the Holy Spirit, it's time you started. I've had great opportunities to tell people about the Holy Spirit in all kinds of situations, even in a swimming pool. They got water baptised at the same time!

Just like God anointed Jesus, He will anoint you with the power of the Holy Spirit to do good, heal the sick and become an advertisement for God in the world. The prophet Joel prophesied: *'And it shall come to pass afterward that I will pour out My Spirit on all flesh; Your sons and your daughters shall prophesy; Your old men shall dream dreams; Your young men shall see visions.'* (Joel 2:28)

When people get saved, praise God that is amazing. But then the work begins. Winning them to the Lord is the easy bit, but building them up, nurturing and discipling them is when the work starts. Those you've led to the Lord are your responsibility, so encourage them, build them up and bring them to church. Help them to read the Word, pray and bring them into an atmosphere where they can grow, develop, and mature. But then God also has another gift: the baptism of the Holy Spirit.

We all start as baby Christians, but God doesn't want us to stay there. He expects us to grow up spiritually. As we grow, there's a changeover point when we become a Christ-centred Christian, putting God and his plan first in our lives.

Our love walk is especially important in ministry too. Once you begin to work with people in ministry, you'll find that others don't always do things as you would. There will be plenty of opportunities to demonstrate your love walk. Remember to walk in love and totally obey the word. Jesus said: *'Love your neighbours, love your enemies, love one another, husbands love your wives, wives respect your husbands.'* Whatever people say or do, you need to make the decision to love them just like God loves them. That's tough in some environments!

Praise God for the day of Pentecost, when the church was born. There was Peter, full of the Holy Spirit on his first preaching engagement, when 3000 people got saved. What a sermon it must have been! This was the public start of the church, when everybody spoke in tongues and all the people around heard them.

God chose Jesus as head of the church. We are the body and He is the head, the architect, the CEO, the founder. There is only one worldwide church and only one owner. Jesus has been building the body, the church worldwide for 2000 years. The Bible says that the gates of Hades will not come against it. There are churches being planted all over the world. And Jesus is the Master Planner with a master plan. He is the King of kings and Lord of lords. He is the Alpha and Omega. He is the King. He is building His church and no demon in hell will prevail against it.

The church is made up of people. It's not about bricks, mortar and nice buildings. Some people have church in the open air. We used to have church under the bridge for our Diamond Project in Indonesia and under trees in Indian villages. Churches have been started or pioneered from small groups, often in people's homes, as ours did. Every church starts small, even the mega churches with up to 40,000 people. Everybody has an opportunity to start a church where they are. Jesus said: *'I will build My church. And the gates of hell will not come against it.'* So, praise God, the church is on the move around the globe.

It's important that we see the big picture: Jesus is coming back soon, for the body of believers worldwide. It won't matter what language you speak or what culture you embrace; it won't matter if you're fat or skinny, old or young, male or female. Jesus is coming back for the whole body of Christ, the universal church. I believe that we can have peace in our heart and mind. We don't have to worry about whether we're building the church because Jesus is building the church.

Prayer: Thank you, Lord, that you are building Your church and the *'gates of hell will not come against it.'* Please fill me afresh with your Holy Spirit so that I can be more effective as a co-worker with Christ in your universal church. Help me to *'make disciples of all nations'* and encourage newborn Christians to receive Your Holy Spirit power in their own lives. And above all, help me to walk in love in all that I do. I ask this in your name, Lord Jesus. Amen.

7
GO INTO ALL THE WORLD

Many people take part in or support short-term missions, but there are some that are called to long-term missions. You can often see them on short trips; they are more likely to be the ones who say: 'I could do this every day for the rest of my life' rather than 'I hate it here! I hate the heat, I hate the food, I want to go home!'

There's a lot more to travelling overseas than you think. The travelling ministry is a multi-task ministry involving huge cultural change, being away from family and friends and being strangers in a foreign land. But if you are called to this, you don't have to be fearful. God will give you a special grace to overcome some of the cultural difficulties. Remember, when you go on the mission field, you're a missionary. You're not part of their nation, whichever nation you go to. There is some understanding with that and they will accept it. It's easier sometimes, as a foreigner in another country, to minister to people because they will receive you more readily, even if you make mistakes.

As a long-term missionary, there will be a lot more to consider than a short trip. You need a continuing supply of resources to cover basic expenses and allow you to undertake God's plan. You need somewhere to live, travelling expenses, excess baggage allowance for books, utilities, clothes, education, petrol, insurance. They all need paying for on the mission field.

It's very important to enter long-term debt free, otherwise you could become a burden to your church, friends and family. Sometimes people have to go back to their homeland and maybe there's some self-financing to do.

Family members are probably the number one supporters of people who go on the mission field. A lot of people look at churches to be the number one supplier. Wrong! Churches are not the number one supplier of finances, but individual people are. There are a few bigger organisations or churches that send missionaries out with an allowance for all living expenses, but most overseas missionaries live by faith and raise their own finances.

A lot of people talk about raising finances or raising support. I now call it raising people. We're talking about raising a group of people who trust you as a missionary, who have the same vision as you and then when you approach them for finances, they say: 'How much do you want?'

It is important to build and maintain those supporters. You need to connect with like-minded people who support in many different ways. I asked a friend of mine to come on a mission trip to share his testimony and he said: 'That's not my calling, Steve. My calling is to be a very good businessman, so that I can support your ministry.'

A lot of people don't like talking about money or asking for it, especially with regard to mission. I encourage you not to be fearful about that. Methods of raising support for short-term and long-term missionaries are different. Long-term support is regular consistent funding, so we need to raise awareness with things like printed material, websites, texts, fridge magnets, photographs, videos, CD's, seasonal cards, charity boxes and giving talks.

Also, report on your ministry regularly, answer questions about finances and ask these people to give to the needed resources.

There are people are out there, waiting for you to share your vision with them. I love it when people come and ask: 'How can I help?' I wouldn't like to have to twist someone's arm until they say yes!

You don't need to be ashamed of receiving money. Some missionaries believe they should live a very simple basic life, settling for holes in their shoes and raggedy, worn tyres on their cars. I don't believe that's how missionaries should live on the mission field. Missionaries and all ministers should live as kings. After all, God calls His children kings and queens, part of His royal family. Ministers are children of God too, and therefore they also are kings and queens, priests of the Lord. You are an ambassador, a labourer for God. When people give you money, they are investing in what God has called you to do.

Remember that we don't have to worry about money! God is our Provider. He is our All-Sufficient One! God never runs out of money. He never runs out of resources. If it's God's will, then it's God's bill. It's the same as a large business. Employees don't have to worry about where the chairs come from, or the notebooks, pens, computers and desks. That's the CEO's responsibility to provide everything that they need to do the job. It's the same with God. When it's our plan, we pay. When it's God's plan, He pays.

Remember, we are all part of the Great Commission, so pray about your part in both long-term and short-term mission and be prepared to go wherever He sends you!

Prayer: Lord, thank you for opportunities to bring the Good News in parts of the world that have never heard about Jesus. Please tell me what part you want me to play in this, whether it's to go out as a missionary or to support one with finances, resources and prayer. Help me to be obedient and go wherever you send me, enabling me to live an extraordinary life and experience the Favour of God. I ask this in the name of Jesus. Amen.

8
ARISE, SHINE, FOR YOUR LIGHT HAS COME

ARISE- GOD IS WITH YOU!

We have seen that we must arise and get out and about to be seen. Often that is not very easy on our flesh, but the good news is that we are never alone. God is always with us in the form of the Holy Spirit! He helps us to fulfil His plan on this earth.

'*Now begin the work, and the Lord be with you.*' (1 Chronicles 22:16).

David is instructing his son Solomon to build the temple. A great task and he needed to know that God was with him. Today, we don't have a temple made out of stones, but with people. In 1 Corinthians 6:19, it says: '*Do you not know that your body is a temple of the Holy Spirit, who is in you, whom you have received from God? You are not your own*'

Prayer: Father, thank you that You are always with me through Your Holy Spirit. Thank You that I don't have to be afraid of man or anything else because You are with me. You are always on my side and together with You I want to build your temple. Thank You that I am part of that temple, but also that I can help building that temple. In Jesus' mighty name. Amen!

ARISE – ABOVE SIN

'Do not gloat over me, my enemy! Though I have fallen, I will rise. Though I sit in darkness, the Lord will be my light.' (Micah 7:8).

God doesn't promise us that we will not fall or that we will never have problems, but He tells us that we can always rise up again and that He will always be our light. All of us make mistakes, but what do we do with them? Are we trying to hide them or even continue doing them? God is very clear in His word. Sin separates man from God and it hinders us to do what He called us to do.

'Therefore, since we are surrounded by such a great cloud of witnesses, let us throw off everything that hinders and the sin that so easily entangles. And let us run with perseverance the race marked out for us' (Hebrews 12:1).

'If we confess our sins, He is faithful and just to forgive us our sins, and to cleanse us from all unrighteousness.' (1 John 1:9)

That is what we should do if we have sin in our lives, so that we can arise again. Don't play with sin and don't nurture thoughts that are not godly. Meditate on God's word and check every thought if it's worthy to be thought of or not. How? Look at Philippians 4:8: *'Finally, brothers and sisters, whatever is true, whatever is noble, whatever is right, whatever is pure, whatever is lovely, whatever is admirable—if anything is excellent or praiseworthy—think about such things.'*

Thoughts are like seeds planted into our minds. Whenever we start meditating on them, they will produce fruit. It's up to us if we water good or bad thoughts. In Philippians 4 we see seeds that will produce good fruit!

Prayer: Thank you Father that You want me to arise when I fall and to be in the light and not in the darkness. Thank You that You are the Father of light, and that there is no darkness in You. I want to ask You to forgive me from (confess to Him your wrongdoings). I want to start thinking only good thoughts and meditate only on the things that pass the test in Philippians 4:8. Holy Spirit I ask You to remind me of this if I meditate on the wrong things. In Jesus' mighty name. Amen!

SHINE – BY BEING WISE AND UNDERSTAND GOD'S PERFECT WILL

At this very season, there is a divine task for each one of us to shine forth the Lord Jesus' glory in the midst of a crooked and perverse generation. To shine means to give out light, to be bright or to reflect light. In Daniel 12:3 it says, *'That those who are wise shall shine like the brightness of the firmament, and those who turn many to righteousness like the stars forever and ever.'*

Daniel 12:10 says, *'Thus, many shall be purified, made white and refined. But the wicked shall do wickedly, and none of the wicked shall understand, but the wise shall understand.'*

We are in the last days, surrounded by sin- internet pornography, drug, and alcohol addiction, adultery, nicotine, divorce. However, since God gave us understanding, we can demonstrate His perfect will to the world. The world views those sins as part of the new trends and choice of lifestyle in the modern age. Sadly, many Christians have also fallen into the trap of the devil without realizing it.

This is the time and the hour for Christians to arise and shine through the help of the Holy Spirit, by being wise, understanding God's perfect will and being aware of all the lies and schemes of the devil.

Prayer: Dear Father, thank you that Your mighty hand has set me from _____ (acknowledge your hindrances, sin, struggle). I allow You to purify, mould, and refine me to be used as your bright star that shines forth Your Glory. Help me to seek Your face and to fear You more than ever before. Thank you for Your wisdom and understanding. In Jesus' mighty name I pray. Amen!

SHINE – AS PURE GOLD

The temple of God, during the leadership of King Solomon, was built by using pure gold (1 Kings 6:19-22). The entire temple was overlaid with pure gold. Both then and now, pure gold is very expensive and a symbol of high quality. Some characteristics of pure gold are soft, pliable, highly valued, shining and glorious. In the New Testament, the temple of God is residing in the body of the believer who has been redeemed by the priceless and precious blood of Jesus.

Jesus is the Lord who searches the mind and the heart of each individual. He knows His very own people. To build the glorious temple, He Himself will cleanse, sanctify, design, and build each individual temple uniquely with His own mighty hand. Each one of us has to present the pure gold in our inner most being for the Most High God.

Pure gold inside of us should be:
- The genuine faith that will not perish. While it is tested by many fires, it should result in praise, honour and glory to God.
- The shining characters that are reflecting the light of Christ.

Prayer: Dear Father, thank you that You value me highly. Now I allow You to remove from my life that which is not honourable before You. Cleanse me, sanctify me, mould me and use me as the glorious temple. I also pray that Your mighty hand may guide me to have genuine faith while I am experiencing various trials. Let all that is in me be as pure gold is before You. Thank you, Father. In Jesus' mighty name. Amen!

SHINE – AS THE SUN

'What sunshine is to flowers, smiles are to humanity. They are but trifles, to be sure but, scattered along life's pathway, the good they do is inconceivable.'

(unknown)

God wants each one of us to shine forth as the sun in the kingdom of the Father (Matthew 13:43). Shine forth as the sun means that we should:

Acknowledge the small things we can do for others (i.e. sincere smiles, having positive faith, encouragement, comforting, appreciation, motivation, forgiveness, praise, thankful heart, patience etc).

Be faithful in whatever we do. In times of trials, we do not quit trying.

'But we should not lose heart in well-doing, for in due season we shall reap, if we do not faint.' (Galatians 6:9)

Be gracious and merciful to others just like God is merciful to us.

'For the Lord is our sun and shield; the Lord will give grace and glory; and there is not one good thing that He will withhold from those who walk uprightly.' (Psalm 84:11)

As we shine forth like the sun, God tells us in Isaiah 60:3: 'And the nations shall come to your light, and kings to the brightness of your dawning.' And Isaiah 60:5, *'Then you shall fear and become bright, and your heart shall throb and swell for joy; because the abundance of the sea shall turn to you, the wealth of the nations will come to you.'* It is indeed when we obey God, we will be blessed beyond measure according to His promises in His word.

Prayer: Father, please forgive me when I may not have been sensitive toward someone else's needs. I may fall short of many things, but it is in Your word that *'The righteous shall shine forth as the sun in the Kingdom of their Father.'*

Regardless of the circumstances Lord, I will arise and shine forth like the sun wherever I am. Thank you for Your grace and mercy that endures forever. In Jesus' mighty name, I pray. Amen!

SHINE – AS WE TRUST AND RELY UPON GOD

Many times in our lives we experience difficulties, insecurities, uncertainties and fear. God sees us through all the seasons of our lives. When the answer or help from the Lord has not yet come, keep trusting and do not give up. We know there is light at the end of the tunnel. God wants us to trust in His Name and rely upon Him. We can trust and rely on God only if we understand who God is. He is our Father, our Provider and our Protector, our Healer, our Saviour, our Helper.

Likewise, Moses, relied on God when he experienced challenges as a leader. He went up to Mount Sinai and when he came down from Mount Sinai, Moses did not know that the skin of his face shone.

'Now it was so, when Moses came down from Mount Sinai (and the two tablets of the Testimony were in Moses' hand when he came down from the mountain), that Moses did not know that the skin of his face shone while he talked with Him.' (Exodus 34:29)

God's Holy Spirit inside of us will open the eyes of our understanding upon the faithfulness and the goodness of God. Moreover, the peace of God that surpasses all understanding will protect us from any fear and anxieties. This is the confidence that we have, that God hears and answers our prayers. As we seek Him, He will deliver us from all our fears.

When we look to Him, we will be radiant since He is merciful to us and His desire is to bless us. He will cause His face to shine upon us (Numbers 6:24-25). Thus, as we all fear Him and know that His name is *'I Am who I Am'* we should trust in the name of the Lord and rely upon Him, throughout our everyday walk.

Prayer: Father, as I draw closer to You, help me to be still and know that You are God. Your Name is *'I Am who I Am'*. I will trust You Lord and rely upon You, regardless of the circumstances in my life. Thank you for Your goodness. Each time I need You, You are always there for me and hear my prayer. I love You Lord. I give You all the fear that I have, such as (confess your fear). I believe that as I seek Your face, You will cause my heart to be filled with Your peace, joy and righteousness. Let mercy, favour and blessings be our banner Lord. In Jesus' mighty name, we pray. Amen!

LIGHT – JESUS IS THE LIGHT OF THE WORLD

The Gospel of John shows us clearly that Jesus Christ is the Light: *'In Him was life, and the life was the light of men.'* (John 1:4) The epistle of John shows us some characteristics of God or the Light: *'And this is the message, which we have heard from Him and declare to you, that God is light and in Him is no darkness at all.'* (1 John 1:5)

'The true light that gives light to everyone was coming into the world. (John 1:9) and *'the darkness couldn't overtake the light.* (John 1:5) Why did God need to reveal His light and overcome darkness? The answer is also found in the His Word: *'Through the tender mercy of our God; by which the Dayspring from on high has visited us, to give light to those who sit in darkness and in the shadow of death, to guide our feet into the way of peace.'* (Luke 1:78-79).

In the Greek ειρήνη (with our letters eirēnē), doesn't just mean to have peace, but also prosperity. Jesus didn't just set us free from the bondage of darkness but sent us into the light to *'to guide our feet into the way of... peace, quietness, rest and also prosperity.'* Eirēnē also means 'set at one again.'

Are we whole again? Do we still have areas in our lives where we don't have peace and rest? The Word of God promises us prosperity in every area of our lives. We all have areas in our lives with a potential to grow, develop and mature, to be more enlightened or filled with His light! Jesus Christ is the Light that can and will enlighten every area that is open to Him. It is up to us to fully open the door so the light can get in!

Prayer: Father reveal to me all the areas that I still have closed and the doors I still haven't fully opened. Give me the strength to open these doors fully and let Your light in. I decide now and here to open all the doors! Reveal to me the plans for all areas of my life. I want to know your plans, purpose and vision for my life. Lord, enter in all the rooms of my life. They all belong to You. In Jesus' mighty name I pray. Amen!

LIGHT – TURN TO THE LIGHT AND WALK IN IT SO THE SHADOWS WILL BE BEHIND YOU

We have seen in the Word of God that Jesus is the light. This light has put away all darkness and is now guiding our feet into the way of peace, rest and prosperity so we can be whole in all areas of our lives.

The question now is, how to receive this light that can do all these remarkable things. John 8:12 has the answer: *'Then Jesus spoke again to them, saying, "I am the Light of the world. He who follows Me shall not walk in darkness but shall have the light of life."'* (John 8:12)

It is on us to follow Jesus so we can have the light. No other can give us this light but only He can, because He Himself is the light. To follow Him and to walk in His light will give us the key to success. We are born again, but we are still living in a dirty world with a lot of challenges. We may be in His light but is His light also in us?

He will be in front of us showing us the way. His way. If we believe in Jesus, we will follow Him and we will become more like Him. There is no other way to get the light than to fully trust in Him and His way for our lives.

'Then Jesus said to them, "Yet a little while the Light is with you. Walk while you have the Light, lest darkness come upon you. For he who walks in darkness does not know where he goes. While you have the Light, believe in

the Light so that you may become sons and daughters of Light." Jesus spoke these things and departed and was hidden from them.' (John 12:35-36)

We always walk! The question is in what direction? How often do we try to get our own way and trust our own knowledge rather than in the light? Since we are born again, we live in Him, but that doesn't settle it.

'If we live in the Spirit, let us also walk in the Spirit.' (Galatians 5:25)

Prayer: Father, I am ready to grow! I want to change whatever has to be changed and go wherever You are telling me to go. I will go step by step and I know that You will guide me in the right direction. Lord I trust You and I will follow You all the days of my life, day by day. In Jesus' mighty name. Amen!

LIGHT – WE HAVE TO PUT ON THE ARMOUR OF LIGHT

Light has been made to be seen. In Matthew 5:15 it says: *'Neither do people light a lamp and put it under a bowl. Instead they put it on its stand, and it gives light to everyone in the house.'*

Why does it have to be seen? Paul writes: *'And persuading yourselves to be a guide of the blind, a light to those in darkness.'* (Rom 2:19).

This light is given to us not just for peace, rest and prosperity, but also to *'guide the blind.'* We see that also in the Gospel of Luke: *'A light for revelation to the nations, and the glory of Your people Israel.'* (Luke 2:32).

The light removes the darkness and it reveals the truth. The truth will set the people free. (John 8:32)

But how will this light be a revelation to the people in darkness? By the glory of His people. In 1 Peter 2:9 we read: '... *so that you might speak of the praises of Him who has called you out of darkness into His marvellous light.'*

People will recognise Him in us because we praise Him and give the honour and praise to Him so that He might be glorified: '*Let your light so shine before men that they may see your good works and glorify your Father who is in Heaven.'* (Matthew 5:16)

The light of God has to be seen. It will be seen through us by all the people who are in darkness. This light will be a guide for them. But this all starts by the decision to step into being a light, by beginning to praise His mighty works and not ours.

'*The night is far spent, the day is at hand; therefore, let us cast off the works of darkness, and let us put on the armour of light.'* (Romans 13:12).

Prayer: Father, I decide right now to praise You with all that I am and give You the honour, glory and praise, so that You are glorified in my life. Your light shall be seen in my life and people shall see Your success in me. In Jesus' name. Amen.

LIGHT – THE GREATEST GLIMPSE OF LIGHT IS LOVE

God is love and love is the ultimate way. Paul says: '*And yet I will show you the most excellent way.'* (1 Corinthians 12:31)

'*Yet I am writing you a new command; its truth is seen in him and in you, because the darkness is passing and the true light is already shining. Anyone who claims to be in the light but hates a brother or sister is still in the darkness. Anyone who loves their brother and sister lives in the light and there is nothing in them to make them stumble. But anyone who hates a brother or sister is in the darkness and walks around in the darkness. They do not know where they are going, because the darkness has blinded them.'* (1 John 2:8-11)

The name 'Christian' wasn't given to the Church members by the apostles, but by the heathens who recognized the people as followers of Christ. How do people know you're a Christian?

'By this shall all men know that you are my disciples, if you have love one to another' (John 13:35).

If we honour God and our siblings, we can and will be a light for the glory of the Lord that will be seen by the people in the darkness and give them opportunity to see the light and to be set free. We don't have to do that by ourselves but by the love of the Lord that was given to us.

'Be kind to one another with a brother's love, putting others before yourselves in honour.' (Rom 12:10)

Prayer: Father, I declare that Your love dwells in me and I am led by Your Spirit to honour You and my brothers and sisters more than I honour myself. Lord I live for Your glory. That's my honour. In Jesus' mighty name I pray. Amen!

LIGHT – WE ARE OF GOD; BORN IN HIS NATURE AS CHILDREN OF LIGHT

We are made in the image and likeness of God and made fully new. Therefore, we are new creatures in Him (2 Corinthians 5:17). We are ambassadors of God who are representing Him in His glory with the light given to us by His redemptive work:

'*You are all the sons of light and the sons of the day. We are not of the night, or of darkness.*' (1 Thessalonians 5:5)

'*You are the light of the world.*' (Matthew 5:14)

'*For you were once darkness, but now you are light in the Lord; walk as children of light.*' (Ephesians 5:8)

In the epistle of Peter we see that there is an even greater dimension of being a light: '*But you are a chosen generation, a royal priesthood, a holy nation, a people for possession, so that you might speak of the praises of Him who has called you out of darkness into His marvellous light.*' (1 Peter 2:9)

We are not just in His light and have become the children of light by accident. We don't have to try to be a light, because if we follow the Lord and put on the armour of light (by decision), then we are the light.

A fish can swim from his nature and if this fish has a baby, their offspring will be a fish too, with the ability to swim. The same with an eagle that can fly and a monkey that can climb. These babies, who have their abilities at birth, only need to learn to develop them as they grow. Now look at God the Almighty One. He has a child. What do you think will this child be and what would this child be able to do?

'*I have said, "You are gods; and all of you sons and daughters of the Most High!"*' (Psalm 82:6)

'*I can do all things through Christ who strengthens me.*' (Philippians 4:13)

Prayer: I declare that am a child of God; chosen by the Master. I am a royal priest, holy and called to speak of the praises of Him! In Jesus' mighty name. Amen.

8.
THE GLORY OF HE
LORD RISES UPON YOU

GLORY – CONSUMED WITH A ZEAL FOR GOD'S GLORY

'....and the glory of the Lord rises upon you.' (Isaiah 60:1).

Ever since the great missionary movement of the gospel that began in the book of Acts, this prophecy is being fulfilled. Christ is the Glory of His people.

Paul and Silas faced a lot of opposition by people during those times who were threatened by this spiritual 'movement' and accused those involved saying: *'These men who have caused trouble all over the world have now come here.'* (Acts 17:6). They surely didn't intend it as a compliment but strangely enough, it was a rather accurate statement! It seems the early church as a whole was consumed with a zeal for God's glory! We are part of that Church today and as the body of Christ we must not do as the Israelites did who lost enthusiasm concerning the glory of God.

Prayer: Dear Heavenly Father, help me not to become complacent about Your glory. Let me always be seen on the forefront in terms of being on fire with God's power and glory, to really turn the world upside down and become a history maker for the gospel and reaching the lost and dying of this world. In Jesus' wonderful name I pray. Amen!

GLORY- REVELATION AND CHANGE

'and the glory of the Lord rises up on you.' (Isaiah 60:1)

In Hebrew God's glory describes the form in which Jehovah (Yahweh) reveals Himself or is the sign and manifestation of His presence. Throughout history God has been faithful to manifest His glory on behalf of His people and we also observe that when the glory of God was in manifestation, it was always a time of revelation and change. We must get a revelation of what God wants us to do.

The Israelites became apathetic in rebuilding God's temple. They became more interested in their own home and everyday business (Haggai 1:2-4). If we are not careful, we too can become more involved with our personal lives than with the things of God. Spiritual things are no longer a priority. We are more interested in furthering ourselves than furthering God's plan and his work.

Prayer: Father forgive me for not always putting You and Your will first in my life. Help me to change my attitude and to let go of some things I have been holding on to, afraid of losing some earthly benefits. Let me count everything else as worthless in comparison to

Your glory manifested in our midst. In Jesus' mighty and abundant name. Amen.

GLORY – FROM GLORY TO GLORY

'....and the glory of the Lord rises up on you.' (Isaiah 60:1)

What is the role of the individual in receiving the glory (manifestation) of the Lord?

'And we all, who with unveiled faces contemplate the Lord's glory, are being transformed into his image with ever-increasing glory, which comes from the Lord, who is the Spirit.' (2 Corinthians 3:18)

The phrase 'changed from glory to glory' implies that there is an ever-present action taking place. The change has to start in our own hearts. The more we get to know the Lord as we walk with Him, the more we will be transformed with His ever-increasing glory.

It is important for each believer to take his place in the church and our individual responsibility in receiving God's glory. We have to move into a position where we can change. We can't be complacent, just sitting in our pews on Sunday mornings, content with status quo and expect to experience revival.

Prayer: Father, help me not to be ignorant or unwilling of what You want me to do in the Church to usher in revival. We want to go from glory to glory. Help us to draw near to You. In Jesus' mighty name I pray. Amen!

GLORY – THE GREATER GLORY

*The Lord tells us in Haggai 2:9 that: 'The glory of this present house
will be greater than the glory of the former house.'*

There are nine keys that we can practice to gain a greater measure of
the glory of God.

1. **Obedience without compromise**
   We have to obey what He says to do in His word.
   *'Whoever has my commands and obeys them, he is the one who
   loves me. He who loves me will be loved by my Father, and I too will
   love him and show myself to him.'* (John 14:21).
   Often, we hear God but only partially obey, because we are too
   busy with our own plans.

2. **Drawing near to God**
   We can draw nearer to God experientially.
   We have to have fellowship with Him in our thoughts, our
   attitudes and worship (James 4:8). Meditating on God's Word
   will draw us closer.

3. **Consecration**
   We must consecrate and dedicate ourselves to God in prayer,
   and we must mean it from our heart: *'Not my will but Yours.'*
   (John 3:30)

4. **Walking in unity before God**
   We all need to be in unity, walking in love toward one another
   and esteeming each believer as a valuable member of the body
   of Christ (2 Chronicles 5:13). There is strength in numbers,

especially when there is unity amongst those numbers. There is nothing like being around those of like-minded faith (Acts 4:23). Where there is strife there will be no manifestation of God's presence (James 3:16).

5. Giving thanks to God

Giving thanks is a means of maintaining a Spirit filled life and positioning ourselves to receive God's glory (Ephesians 5:18-20).

6. Giving praise to God

It's not just during the happy moments in life that we are to praise the Lord, but also in our darkest hour- our midnight hour (Acts 16:25-26). Praises ought to come from the heart, something that causes you to lift your hands or fall on your knees in gratitude and in awe of God Himself.

7. Worshipping God

The Bible says that God seeks out those who will worship Him (John 4:23). God delights in manifesting Himself when people are worshipping Him from the depths of their hearts, for who He is and His awesome greatness. It's not just about having a good time at church but rather a true reverence for the Holy One. True worship comes from the heart not from the head! It is the attitude of our heart and our priorities and focus that will determine whether we enter into God's greater glory.

8. Prayer

John Wesley once said: 'It seems that God can do nothing on this earth unless someone asks Him.' God wants us to ask of Him! It is our responsibility as believers to be people of prayer. Real, heartfelt prayer- Bible prayer that will always reap Bible results!

'This is the confidence we have in approaching God: that if we ask anything according to his will, he hears us. And if we know that he hears us—whatever we ask—we know that we have what we asked of him.' (1 John 5:14-15)

9. **Reverence**

   To reverence God doesn't mean we are solemn and sad, but rather yielding and respecting what He wants us to do, and joyfully enter into the flow of His presence in our midst.

Prayer: Father, in the mighty name of Jesus, show me areas in my life where I walk in disobedience that I may not hinder the move of the Holy Spirit. Please forgive me and help me to change whatever needs changing to experience the greater glory of You. Father not my will but Yours in my life. Amen.

Prayer: Father, in the mighty name of Jesus, help me to walk in love and not getting entangled in strife. I thank and praise You for who You are and stand in awe of You. In times when things seem to go wrong, help us to hold on to You. Amen.

'And be not drunk with wine, wherein is excess; but be filled with the Spirit; Speaking to yourselves in psalms and hymns and spiritual songs, singing and making melody in your heart to the Lord; Giving thanks always for all things unto God and the Father in the name of our Lord Jesus Christ.' (Ephesians 5:18-20)

Prayer: Father, please help all of us to establish a lifestyle of giving thanks, praise and worship to You, that we will move closer to experiencing a move of the Holy Spirit in our midst such as we have never seen before and a multiplication of new converts; a harvest beyond measure. I ask this in the mighty name of Jesus. Amen.

Question: Do you think that your name is written in the Lamb's Book of Life in pencil? And God's got a big eraser in His hand ready to just wipe you out? No! Your name is written in the Lamb's Book of Life by the blood of Jesus Christ. The Greater One, the Holy Spirit, is living on the inside of you and me. He is greater than all the storms of life. He is greater than leprosy. He is greater than blindness. He is even greater than death. He said: '*Lazarus, come forth,*' and Lazarus, who was dead, came forth bound hand and foot with grave clothes. God is greater than the storm. He said: 'Peace, be still,' and there was a great calm. He is the Greater One! Greater than the devil and demons! Greater than sickness and disease! Greater than all the temptations and tests of life! He is living in me and He is living in you!

What is He doing in you? He is in you to help you. He is in you to strengthen you. He is in you to lift you up. He is in you to make you an overcomer. He is in you to make you a success and make you a victorious, Christ-centred Christian.

And God, this indescribable, amazing, incredible, awesome God wants you to work for Him and be His ambassador to speak for Him, going to a lost and dying world. Wow, what a privilege! I challenge you and dare you to just do it.

And don't forget, the **Favour of God** (FOG) will follow you all the days of your life.

Get ready, fasten your seatbelts for the best is yet to come as you walk by faith and be led by the Holy Spirit.

God bless you all abundantly and I pray that the **Favour of God** will be on you in every area of your life as you are obedient to him.

Steve

Rev Steve Laidlow
Ordained Minister of the Gospel
Founder of Acorn International Ministries, Yayasan Acorn Indonesia and Life Tributes.
Tel: +44 07469 949851. Email: acornintmin@cfaith.com

A WRITER'S LESSON IN GETTING OUT OF THE BOAT

Back in August 2018, I was approached by a newcomer to our church, who needed help in editing and publishing a book. After reading the proposed contents and gasping in horror at the size of the project– 138,000 words of international sermon transcriptions– I sent him a lengthy list of everything that needed to be done in order to turn it into a readable publication.

'Great,' said Steve Laidlow. 'Let's go for it!'

However, I had no idea that the happy ending to the story I was about to work on would start to unfold before my eyes. I was one of the many who cheered and clapped when our much-loved pastor, Ann Strickland, made the surprise announcement of her engagement to Steve Laidlow at church one Sunday morning (What, that new guy I'm doing the book for? Wow!). I was one of the many celebrating their special day and wiping away tears of joy when listening to the incredible story of how God had brought them together. And, of course, two such extraordinary people had to have an extraordinary love story– meeting at the bus stop just wouldn't have packed the same literary punch!

And then it dawned on me that I was now producing a book for our pastor's husband that a lot of my church family would read. No pressure there then!

But when we finally managed to squeeze in interviews between wedding plans, mission trips and house moves, I sat enthralled as he unpacked the extraordinary events of his story so far and the lessons God has taught him during the eventful journey. And as the book started to take shape, those lessons started to impact my own life as God spoke to me during the editing process.

The truth is that this has been the most challenging writing project I've ever worked on. I told God that I would do it if He wanted me to and then repeatedly changed my mind! My cry of: 'Lord, it's too hard, pick someone else,' became a regular prayer-time grumble. But the lessons learned through the 'stretch and challenge' I was fighting against were priceless. That indescribable joy of working through God's plan for your life and seeing it come to fruition is an incredible feeling. It always feels like Christmas has arrived early- that's the only way I can describe it! But it's a feeling that I never would have experienced had I remained in the 'safety' of my comfort zone.

I can personally testify that **The Favour of God** really does descend on your life when you push aside fear and 'step out of the boat' in obedience to Him. I pray that the contents of this book will impact your own life in an even greater measure.

Who needs mediocre when we have amazing to aim for!

Andi Robinson

Andi Robinson is a freelance writer and author based in Blackpool, North West England. Previous books include the award-winning 'One Step Beyond: One Man's Journey from Near Death to New Life,' the sequel 'It Must Be Love: The Story Continues,' 'What the Dickens' by Albert Dicken and 'The Monster Within' by Brian Greenaway (the sequel to the bestselling 'Hell's Angel').

She can be contacted through her website www.haveigotwordsforyou.com

ONE FINAL THING

We hope that you have enjoyed this book and have been both blessed and inspired. We would be really grateful if you could leave a review for The FOG on Amazon. This will help to encourage people to buy it and receive that blessing for themselves.

May I also ask that if you come across any errors, such as typos, would you let us know? We are a small editorial team (thanks to beta readers Kate Towers, Andrea Branson and Tony Wilson) and we've tried to be as thorough as possible, but mistakes occasionally slip through the proofreading net.

Please message andirobinson.writer@gmail.com.

Thank you for your support and God bless you.

43612670R00107

Printed in Poland
by Amazon Fulfillment
Poland Sp. z o.o., Wrocław